URANIUM, NUCLEAR POWER, AND CANADA-U.S. ENERGY RELATIONS

Hugh C. McIntyre

CANADIAN-AMERICAN COMMITTEE
sponsored by
C. D. Howe Research Institute (Canada)
National Planning Association (U.S.A.)

Legal Deposit — 2nd Quarter 1978
Quebec National Library
Library of Congress Catalogue Number 78-54112
ISBN 0-88806-035-1
78-4931   April, 1978, $4.00
Quotation with appropriate credit is permissible
C. D. Howe Research Institute (Montreal, Quebec) and
National Planning Association (Washington, D.C.)
Printed in Canada

STATEMENT
BY THE CANADIAN-AMERICAN COMMITTEE
ON *Uranium, Nuclear Power, and Canada-U.S. Energy Relations*
by Hugh C. McIntyre

Since its discovery in the late 1940s, many nations have dreamt that controlled nuclear fission would one day be the key to an almost endless stream of low-cost electrical energy that would ensure economic growth and prosperity. The technological advances in the peaceful use of the atom over the past three decades have brought this dream several steps closer to reality; indeed, today nuclear power occupies an ever-increasing role in meeting the energy needs of the Canadian and the U.S. economies.

Yet no other form of energy development has stirred as much controversy as that associated with the commercial development of nuclear power plants. The controversy has intensified of late as nations consider the nuclear option as an alternative to producing electricity from increasingly scarce and expensive fossil fuels. Proponents assert that nuclear power offers a low-cost source of energy that is indispensable to the future of the world economy. Those in opposition argue that it represents an unacceptably dangerous source of energy and point to its potential for environmental damage and to the very serious consequences that could arise from any further proliferation of nuclear weapons.

One of the key areas in the nuclear power controversy concerns the question of whether enough uranium will be available to meet future fuel requirements. The debate, for example, concerning the development of plutonium recycling and the breeder reactor turns on the question of the adequacy of uranium reserves into the next century. Canada and the United States share a mutual interest and concern over the availability of uranium supplies.

The Canadian-American Committee has had a continuing interest in the overall energy situation, and particularly in how it applies to Canada-U.S. relations. Recognizing the importance of nuclear power as a component in this picture, the Canadian-American Committee authorized this study of the outlook for uranium in North America and the implications for Canada-U.S. energy relations. In commissioning this study, the Committee had two basic objectives in mind. First, it felt that there was a clear need for a basic survey that would gather the available facts and spell out the issues in the areas of uranium supply and nuclear power development in such a way as to make them understandable to readers without a technical background. The Committee did not seek to produce an exhaustive study requiring original research and analysis. Rather, it chose to have the author draw upon available research material and conduct interviews with experts in both Canada and the United States. Second, the Committee wanted to explore bilateral options concerning trade in uranium, nuclear power, and technology arising out of the changing patterns of uranium supply and demand in each country. The author chosen for this assignment was Hugh C. McIntyre, a journalist specializing in energy matters.

From his review of the factors expected to influence the uranium market to the end of this century, Mr. McIntyre has arrived at the following general conclusions:

• First, there is some uncertainty as to whether, within the next decade, the United States will be able to meet its total uranium demands from domestic sources of supply.

• Second, Canada's reserves of uranium are sufficient that they could be developed to supply a significant portion of any shortfall in the United States. At present, however, Canadian uranium producers have long-term contracts with European and Japanese buyers for most of their exportable output. If U.S. utilities want access to Canadian uranium in the 1980s, they should begin investigating the formation of partnership arrangements with Canadian interests for the development of new mining capacity.

• Third, in the period after 1985, uranium demand will be greatly influenced by technological developments in the generation of nuclear power, and Canada and the United States should collaborate to as great an extent as possible in investigating these new technologies.

In the Committee's view, an important aspect of this study is that it indicates how critical uranium is to the long-run energy prospects of Canada and the United States. If uranium supplies are insufficient to permit nuclear power to provide its anticipated share of total energy needs, additional pressures will be exerted on other energy sources, some of which are already in short supply. The Committee is concerned that the opportunities to stretch out uranium supplies over the next decade or so are very limited because Canada and the United States will be locked into current technology. Accordingly, the introduction of new, fuel-efficient technologies in a decade's time will be critical if nuclear power is to continue to be an important energy source. For this reason the Committee recommends that both countries give high priority to exploring alternative nuclear power and nuclear fuel options.

The author's analysis and conclusions regarding the outlook for uranium and nuclear power development are his own. As is customary, the Committee does not necessarily endorse them but does recommend the publication of this study in the belief that it offers an intelligent, readable contribution to greater public understanding of a vital aspect of the energy concerns in both countries.

MEMBERS OF THE CANADIAN-AMERICAN COMMITTEE SIGNING THE STATEMENT

Co-Chairmen

ROBERT M. MacINTOSH
Executive Vice-President, The Bank of Nova Scotia

PHILIP BRIGGS
Executive Vice President, Metropolitan Life Insurance Company

Vice-Chairmen

STEPHEN C. EYRE
Comptroller, Citibank, N. A.

ADAM H. ZIMMERMAN
Executive Vice President, Noranda Mines Limited

Members

JOHN N. ABELL
Vice President and Director, Wood Gundy Limited

R. L. ADAMS
Executive Vice President, Continental Oil Company

J. D. ALLAN
President, The Steel Company of Canada, Limited

CHARLES F. BAIRD
President, INCO Limited

IAN A. BARCLAY
Chairman, British Columbia Forest Products Limited

MICHEL BÉLANGER
President and Chief Executive Officer, Provincial Bank of Canada

ROY F. BENNETT
President and Chief Executive Officer, Ford Motor Company of Canada, Limited

ROD J. BILODEAU
Chairman of the Board and Chief Executive Officer, Honeywell Limited

ROBERT BLAIR
President and Chief Executive Officer, Alberta Gas Trunk Line Company Limited

ARDEN BURBIDGE
Park River, North Dakota

NICHOLAS J. CAMPBELL, JR.
New York, New York

*SHIRLEY CARR
Executive Vice-President, Canadian Labour Congress

W. R. CLERIHUE
Executive Vice-President, Corporate Staff, Celanese Corporation

HON. JOHN V. CLYNE
MacMillan Bloedel Limited

THOMAS E. COVEL
Marion, Massachusetts

JOHN H. DICKEY
President, Nova Scotia Pulp Limited

JOHN S. DICKEY
President Emeritus and Bicentennial Professor of Public Affairs, Dartmouth College

THOMAS W. diZEREGA
Vice President, Northwest Pipeline Corporation

WILLIAM EBERLE
Robert Weaver Associates

A. J. FISHER
President and Chairman of the Board, Fiberglas Canada Limited

ROBERT M. FOWLER
Chairman, Executive Committee, C. D. Howe Research Institute

JOHN F. GALLAGHER
Vice President — International Operations, Sears, Roebuck and Company

PAT GREATHOUSE
Vice President, International Union, UAW

JOHN H. HALE
Executive Vice President, Finance, Alcan Aluminium Ltd.

JOHN A. HANNAH
Executive Director, World Food Council — United Nations

ROBERT H. HANSEN
Senior Vice President — International, Avon Products, Inc.

JAMES A. HENDERSON
Executive Vice President, American Express Co.

ROBERT H. JONES
President, The Investors Group

JOSEPH D. KEENAN
President of Union Label Service & Trades Department, AFL-CIO

DONALD P. KELLY
President and Chief Executive Officer, Esmark, Inc.

DAVID KIRK
Executive Secretary, The Canadian Federation of Agriculture

MICHAEL M. KOERNER
President, Canada Overseas Investments Limited

J. L. KUHN
President and General Manager, 3M Canada Limited

*See Footnotes to the Statement, page 68.

CONTENTS

Tables

Figures

Charts

1

Uranium Supply: The Context

Despite the current swirl of controversies about proliferation, reprocessing, and spent-fuel storage, nuclear power is admitted, even by most of its more responsible adversaries, to be a necessary component of North American energy supply well into the twenty-first century. The United States is currently the largest user of nuclear power, and Canada is the largest exporter of uranium for nuclear fuel.

The purpose of this study is to review the outlook for uranium supply and demand with reference to potential U.S. requirements from now to the year 2000 and the extent to which Canadian exportable uranium resources could become an important supplement to U.S. domestic reserves. Since questions of energy policy and new technology have an important impact on these requirements, they are discussed in the context of each nation's involvement with nuclear fuel technology and against the broader background of Canada-U.S. energy relations, which have become a topic of ever-increasing significance to all North Americans.

The Background

After the achievement of controlled nuclear fission in the closing years of World War II, it was widely anticipated that peaceful applications of this immense new energy resource would produce almost unlimited amounts of low-cost electric energy to assure continued world economic growth and progress. By the late 1960s, Canada, the United States, and several European nations had launched successful commercial-scale atomic power programs, and a bountiful future seemed just around the corner.

For a number of reasons, however, that bright nuclear future now seems in jeopardy:

- Heavy capital requirements and lengthy construction times for nuclear facilities have taxed the planning and funding capabilities of utilities.
- Public-interest groups have mounted strong campaigns to subject nuclear projects to close scrutiny on safety and environmental

1

grounds, and public authorities have frequently permitted such pressures to impose extended delays on construction and licensing of planned facilities, further complicating their funding.
- The recent recessionary period has fostered a pessimistic attitude among utility executives about the rate of growth of demand for electricity.
- There is worldwide uncertainty as to whether future supplies of uranium will be sufficient to fuel the nuclear power plants already built, under construction, and projected.

Nowhere are these problems more apparent than in the United States, currently the world's largest producer of nuclear power with about 40 percent of total world capacity. Of 217 nuclear power plants planned for completion over the next decade by U.S. utilities (on January 1, 1977, there were 61 plants in operation), only 73 have received government licences for construction. Construction of the rest has been delayed by public intervention or postponed by the utilities involved. Similar problems have surfaced in Europe, Japan, and Canada, but generally do not appear to be as severe. In Canada, where most utilities are publicly owned, completion dates for two nuclear stations in Ontario and one in Quebec have been set back, largely for financial reasons.

Of all these problems, that of the supply of uranium is undoubtedly the most fundamental. In the United States, diminishing supplies of hydrocarbon fuels and environmental and transportation problems inherent in any massive expansion of coal utilization make it clear that the United States must henceforth rely on nuclear power for an increasing share of its electricity. Present U.S. forecasts for nuclear fuel requirements indicate that known low- and medium-cost domestic reserves will be exhausted well before the end of the century.[1] The nuclear future of the United States is therefore dependent on either discoveries of new uranium deposits or uranium imports.

The U.S. uranium industry — and the Energy Research and Development Administration (ERDA), the agency that, until 1977, when it was incorporated into the new federal U.S. Department of Energy, forecasted nuclear power and uranium requirements — has been operating on the assumption that, should uranium become scarce, spent fuel from U.S. reactors could be processed to extract fissionable plutonium and uranium isotopes and that this material could be refabricated into "recycled" nuclear fuel. This procedure is called "closing the fuel cycle." At the same time, fast-breeder reactors would be developed to use the plutonium recycled from conventional reactors. It was anticipated that in this way the amount of

---

[1] As explained in the course of this study, low- and medium-cost reserves are those deposits of uranium for which the cost of production of uranium oxide (U_3O_8) is less than U.S.$30 per pound.

energy derived from each pound of uranium could be greatly increased. This assumption was challenged by the energy policy announced by President Carter in April, 1977, which stated that the United States would defer indefinitely the commercial reprocessing and recycling of spent fuel, that construction of a prototype, commercial-size fast-breeder reactor would be canceled, and that the U.S. program would be redirected "towards evaluation of alternative breeders, fuel, and advanced converter reactors."[2]

While one cannot argue with the lofty principles of nuclear non-proliferation and energy conservation underlying Carter's policy, his policy does have far-reaching implications for the uranium supply-demand situation in the United States. The decision to proceed indefinitely with an "open" fuel cycle increases projected uranium requirements for the period 1985 to 2000 by foreclosing the implementation of nuclear technology options that would be more uranium-efficient. If expansion of nuclear power is to be one way for the United States to satisfy its future energy needs, the Carter policy increases the likelihood that the uranium requirements to produce this energy will not be available from domestic low- and medium-cost resources.

In contrast to the situation in the United States, Canada could have an exportable surplus of uranium from proven and reasonably assured resources well into the future. Canadian production would be a logical source for a major proportion of U.S. requirements that could not be provided by domestic production. However, Canadian production for U.S. customers would have to come mainly from resources yet to be developed, since existing Canadian exportable resources are largely committed to other, long-term, offshore customers. The principal challenge for Canada-U.S. energy relations with respect to uranium, consequently, is the creation of a mutually beneficial long-term strategy for the development of new uranium resources in Canada.

This study examines various North American uranium supply-demand projections to the end of this century and considers their differences and their implications. The projections are based on current evaluations of uranium resources and on present, as well as possible future, nuclear-power-technology options.

While the need for long-range planning of uranium supplies is the major conclusion of this study, several other specific suggestions for fruitful bilateral cooperation emerge which are worth mentioning at the outset:

• Both countries are presently re-evaluating their structures of federal and local regulation of both nuclear power and uranium min-

---

[2] Fact Sheet released by White House, April 20, as reproduced in *Daily Oil Bulletin*, April 25, 1977, p. 5.

ing in the light of the constraints these regulations have imposed upon the expansion of these industries, and some exchange of information, experience, and intention between the two governments should be useful.

• In the event of a temporary shortfall of electricity-generating capacity in the U.S. Northeast, it might be useful to examine the possibility of moving ahead the schedules of some CANDU reactors planned for southern Ontario and leasing them for a limited period to provide a block of base-load power.

• To replace the breeder reactor as a uranium-economical alternative for the 1990s, Canada and the United States could initiate a joint development program on a heavy-water-moderated, thorium-fueled, "near-breeder" reactor. A logical first step, however, would be an evaluation of the availability and producibility of the required thorium resources of the United States and Canada.

• A more orderly uranium market might be created by the coordination of any national uranium-stockpiling programs. However, such stockpiles could not be expected to buffer possible future price increases. Unlike most major mineral commodities, uranium is marketed on the basis of long-term contracts with provision for price escalation. Stockpiles would be useful only in providing a price floor during periods of slack demand and thus encouraging confidence in developing higher-cost reserves.

A salient fact that cannot be too strongly emphasized is the high degree of uncertainty in both nuclear power projections and uranium resource evaluation. In the following chapters an attempt is made, based on existing published information supplemented by interviews with government and industry authorities in both the United States and Canada, to present these differences and discrepancies in the expectations of demand for both nuclear power and uranium. It has been felt more valuable for this study to suggest a range of probabilities than to select any single set from among these conflicting projections upon which to erect a narrowly based conclusion.

Chapter 2 gives a brief introduction to nuclear power technology, fuel production, and uranium resource development. Chapter 3 indicates major U.S. supply-demand uncertainties both in reserve estimates and actual uranium-production prospects and in the projection of nuclear-reactor electric-power capacity and the rate of its installation over the next twenty-five years. This allows an "envelope" estimate of U.S. uranium requirements in the last two decades of the century, with due allowance for various uncertainties, such as the export position of new producing countries and the question of new separative and reprocessing capacity in the United States.

Chapter 4 considers Canada's position as a uranium exporter, in terms of both forward production estimates and domestic needs, with allowance for special considerations, such as existing commitments, bilateral agreements, and the impact of federal and provincial taxation and regulation of both producers and nuclear electric utilities.

Chapter 5 focuses upon alternative technologies which could be available in the post-1985 period, and upon the impact these might have upon various supply-demand scenarios. Chapter 6 develops some conclusions as to how Canada and the United States, two economies dependent upon nuclear power for an essential part of their energy budgets, might best maintain cooperation in, and mutually benefit from, the exploitation of nuclear technology and materials.

2

Uranium Utilization and Extraction

The technology of conventional power generation has become sufficiently refined over time that the amount of electrical energy producible from a ton of oil or coal can be projected to within a percentage point. Estimates of conventional fuel requirements can be made with considerable accuracy for extended periods, since only small, incremental improvements can be expected in the technology. Justification of fuel choice, equipment, and selection of environmental protection systems can be based, in current dollars, on quite exact figures, although the differential rate of price escalation of various energy commodities still adds an element of uncertainty to even medium-term forecasting.

Nuclear power technology, in contrast, is still in its comparative infancy, since the first prototype nuclear power plants were completed less than twenty years ago. Following World War II, each of the industrialized victors found its way in isolation to nuclear power, so that the U.S., Canadian, British, and French power reactor systems are markedly different in concept and design and reflect such differing national considerations as whether enriched uranium was available to the commercial sector, whether utilities were publicly or privately owned, and whether capital was cheap or expensive. Furthermore, because of the close connection between weapons technology and nuclear power development, considerations of geopolitics and national security had as great an influence on nuclear programs as did questions of commercial viability.

The technological factors that affect uranium supply and demand range from the geology of uranium deposits to the design of nuclear power systems. The economics of uranium discovery, extraction, and use can also be influenced by non-technological factors. For example, the U.S. decision in 1964 to embargo the use of foreign uranium in domestic reactors in order to protect domestic uranium producers slowed the rate of discovery and development of uranium resources in the rest of the world.

This chapter explains how nuclear power is generated, examines the geological factors affecting uranium production, and reviews the course of the uranium market over the past twenty-five years. In the process it attempts to illuminate the complex technical, economic, and political considerations affecting uranium supply and demand.

How Nuclear Power Is Produced

Nuclear power is produced by the splitting, or "fission," of heavy elements under the impact of uncharged nuclear particles called neutrons.[1] Fission produces great quantities of energy which is utilized in a power reactor as heat to boil water and generate electricity.

Of the so-called "fissionable" elements, only uranium is obtainable in nature in large quantities. Moreover, only one natural isotope of uranium, U-235, is fissionable, and U-235 makes up only 0.7 percent of naturally occurring uranium.[2] Uranium consists mostly of the isotope U-238. U-238 is, however, along with another natural element, thorium, what is called "fertile" — that is, it can absorb neutrons when placed inside a reactor and becomes transformed into fissionable material. For instance, U-238 becomes transformed in a series of steps into Plutonium-239, the first-discovered man-made fissionable element.

The great technical problem faced by the pioneers in nuclear energy development was to produce a fission reaction that was self-sustaining, so that neutrons produced by one fission would go on to trigger subsequent fissions. At the same time, the rate of such fissions must not accelerate so rapidly as to produce an uncontrollable nuclear explosion. The United States and Canada adopted very different approaches to solving this problem. The U.S. approach was to "enrich" the uranium fuel by concentrating the fissionable U-235 isotope, so that the nuclear fuel contains roughly 3.0 percent fissionable atoms instead of 0.7 percent. With the higher concentration of fissionable material, it is easier to achieve a self-sustaining nuclear reaction. Enrichment, however, requires very large, complex plants with a high input of electrical energy.

The Canadian approach was to leave the uranium fuel in its natural isotopic state, but to compensate for the scarcity of fissionable atoms, relative to the U.S. system, by slowing down the speed of the neutrons that trigger the fissions. The slower a neutron goes, the greater the chance statistically that it will interact with a fissionable atom before escaping from the reactor core. The neutrons are

---

[1] While it is theoretically feasible to obtain large amounts of energy by fusing together atoms of light elements (called fusion), the technique has so far not been brought into the realm of practicality, and even enthusiastic investigators hope for no more than a successful laboratory prototype within the next generation.

[2] Isotopes are chemically indistinguishable constituents of an element which differ in the number of elementary particles in their nuclei and, therefore, in their nuclear reactions. Each has a distinctive atomic weight and is identified by this number.

slowed down by the use of heavy water as the "moderator" — the material in which the reaction takes place. Both light (that is, ordinary) and heavy water moderate neutrons, but light water absorbs hundreds of times as many, which are lost to the fission reaction. Heavy-water reactors are "neutron economical," losing few neutrons to absorption.

In either type of reactor a second reaction is going on: the absorbing of excess neutrons (two or more are produced in each fission) by U-238 to produce plutonium. Some of this plutonium contributes to the fission process, and some is left in the used fuel when it is discharged from the reactor core. Because a certain concentration of fissionable atoms is required to sustain the fission reaction, it will be appreciated that a substantial amount of fissionable material always remains in used nuclear fuel.

The most widely employed types of nuclear power reactors in the United States are the boiling-water reactor (BWR) and the pressurized-water reactor (PWR). In the former, the moderator, which is also the coolant,[3] is water that is allowed to boil until it becomes high-pressure steam that is then used directly to drive turbine generators. In the pressurized-water reactor, high-pressure water is used to remove heat from the reactor core and is then passed through heat exchangers to provide steam for the generators. Both BWRs and PWRs are generically termed "light-water reactors" (LWRs).

The most common type of Canadian reactor — the CANDU — is similar to the PWR, except that the coolant and moderator is heavy water in a pressurized closed circuit which produces steam in a separate light-boiling-water circuit. In contrast to the U.S. reactors, the CANDU system uses pressure tubes to contain the fuel and coolant so that nuclear fuel bundles can be added continuously during operation. This is called "on-power refueling." U.S. reactors have the entire core surrounded by a pressure vessel and must be shut down periodically for reloading.

A third type of reactor, the fast-breeder reactor, is of possible future importance. It uses highly enriched fuel and does not employ a moderator to slow down the neutrons. Sufficient fast neutrons interact with the highly enriched fuel to support a chain reaction, and fast neutrons are more effective in converting fertile materials to fissionable materials. The theory of operation is that for each fission at least one neutron is absorbed by fertile material, such as U-238, in the fuel, which is converted into plutonium, and that in operation the reactor "breeds" a greater amount of fissionable material than is consumed. The fuel cycles for the three types of reactors are diagrammed in Figure 1.

---

[3] The "coolant" is the working medium of the power plant, transferring heat energy from the core to the electric generating system.

FIGURE 1

Fuel Cycles of Three Basic Reactor Types

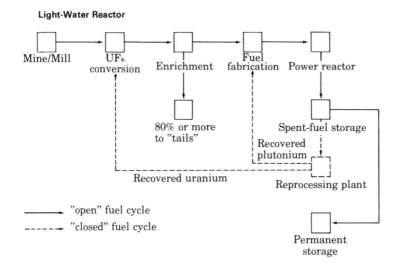

Light-Water Reactor

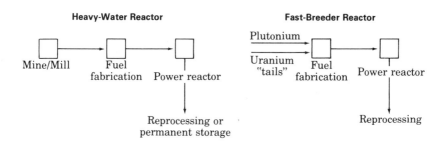

The type of reactor used has definite implications for uranium requirements. With respect to reactors currently in commercial operation in Canada and the United States, it would seem safe to say that the natural uranium system is about 30 percent more uranium-economical.[4] This economy is counterbalanced in higher capital costs per installed megawatt in the CANDU system. Breeder reactors could bring about far greater efficiencies of fuel use, but their development has been hampered by various problems.

[4] Report of the Workshop on Alternative Energy Strategies (WAES), *Energy: Global Prospects 1985-2000*, Carroll L. Wilson, Director (New York: McGraw-Hill, 1977), p. 214. The 30 percent figure is intermediate between the fuel "burn-up" now experienced by U.S. power reactors in service and that projected for newly designed reactors.

Early models of the fast-breeder reactor, such as the Enrico Fermi power plant outside Detroit, demanded too much of current materials technology. That reactor is at present closed down and inoperable. Though proponents of the idea, including many prominent nuclear scientists, argued that within a few decades breeder reactors would provide nuclear fuel for an infinite period of time, this alternative has been ruled out for the near term by the new direction given to U.S. energy policy by President Carter. Private industry lacks the resources to develop the breeder concept, and although there are promising European prototypes, even France, the leader in this technology, has only very recently approved the start of construction on a 1000-megawatt prototype, called Super Phenix, which could eventually generate power for commercial purposes. The generation of such fissionable material as plutonium by chemical reprocessing of fuel has become highly controversial because the process is similar to that used to make material for nuclear weapons, because the used material that must be handled is highly radioactive, and because plutonium itself, as well as being potentially explosive, is extremely radioactive. Considering the number of nations routinely extracting plutonium for military purposes, and the concern in many quarters about where the supply to meet a rising demand will come from, it seems likely that, with due attention to safety and security precautions, large-scale reprocessing of nuclear fuel will take place in time. In the United States, however, the policy of the Carter Administration will extend this time span considerably.

In addition to the reactors that have been discussed, there are other technological options that could influence fuel efficiency. A different "breeding" cycle, using a mixture of thorium and uranium, which can be employed with CANDU reactors is capable of enormously extending uranium supplies. This system is discussed in some detail in Chapter 5. It has also been found that the addition of a very small amount of plutonium to natural uranium fuel (about one part in 1,000) doubles the amount of energy that can be extracted from natural uranium fuel. Finally, under the Carter policy, the U.S. nuclear research program is to be redirected towards an examination of alternative "advanced-converter" technologies. Advanced-converter reactors, of which the CANDU is considered to be one, utilize a higher proportion of their fissionable fuel than present light-water reactors. Attempts in the United States to develop another form of advanced converter — a high-temperature, gas-cooled reactor — have run into engineering problems, and no new versions of this type of reactor are being built.

The Question of Reserves

The nature of uraniferous ores and the manner in which they are deposited provide important insights into the factors affecting the cost and the availability of uranium.

Uranium is an element that is relatively scarce in the earth's crust, and it is widely diffused because, under the right conditions of temperature and geochemistry, it is soluble in water. The oceans, for instance, have been estimated to contain 4,000 times as much uranium as exists in all known ore bodies. Uranium's comparative rarity, however, does not mean that it is difficult to find and extract economically. Tin and silver are both less abundant, yet have been extensively mined since the dawn of history. The cost of economic recovery of any element is a function of its concentration in a particular medium. Hence, it has been uneconomic to attempt recovery from the oceans, where its concentration is of the order of 2 parts per million, while commercial extraction of land deposits has been extensive. Both Canada and the United States have substantial uranium deposits. Known reserves in the United States are in the order of 600,000 tons of uranium oxide (U_3O_8) and, in Canada, about 440,000 tons.[5] Canada has already produced 120,000 tons of uranium, most of which has been exported. As will become evident in the next chapter, these are rough figures and, to be meaningful, need to be accompanied by estimates of cost, probability, and producibility.

According to the most generally accepted theory, uranium deposits were first formed when the earth's atmosphere was almost devoid of oxygen. With the evolution of plant life during the pre-Cambrian era, 2.2 billion years ago, the earth's present oxygen-rich atmosphere resulted. The uranium-containing compounds became water-soluble in the "oxidizing" environment. Unless they were buried at greater depths in the earth, or at the bottom of sea sediments, they were dissolved. However, they were re-precipitated wherever they encountered "reducing" conditions in underground structural "traps." When protected from further leaching by ground water, such concentrations were preserved; otherwise, they were washed deeper into the earth or into the sea. Some uranium deposits are believed to have been dissolved and redeposited several times.[6]

Uranium in exploitable concentrations exists in four major types of deposits in North America: quartz-pebble conglomerates of great age (as at Elliot Lake, Canada); in lenses and rolls in sandstone formations (as in the western United States); in pitchblende, vein-type deposits (as in the Beaverlodge deposit in Saskatchewan); and in pegmatite masses in the granite of the Canadian Shield. The geology of uranium deposits is significant in the Canada-U.S. context in two respects. First, prospective areas of uranium deposits are much larger in extent in Canada, with commercial discoveries

---

[5] Uranium is most frequently measured in terms of U_3O_8. Following its removal from the mine, uranium ore, which may contain as little as 0.1 percent U_3O_8, is milled to produce "yellowcake," a concentrate containing about 80 percent U_3O_8.

[6] For a more detailed discussion see J. H. Tatsch, *Uranium Deposits* (Sudbury, Mass.: Tatsch Associates, 1976).

stretching from the western border of Saskatchewan to the coast of Labrador, while all U.S. commercial discoveries have been in the western sedimentary basin in an arc from Texas to Montana. Second, the nature of the deposits in Canada tends to facilitate larger-scale mining operations than those in the United States.

Except for the Elliot Lake conglomerates, which are of considerable extent and in which reserves have been proven sufficient to last well into the 21st century at present rates of production, other types of exploitable deposits in North America tend to be small but rich (and are usually surrounded by masses of lower-grade ore). This is graphically exhibited in the recent Key Lake find in Saskatchewan, where 50 million pounds of uranium exist in a deposit about 660 feet by 100 feet, nowhere more than 70 feet in thickness — about the size of a medium-sized office building. One experienced uranium prospector characterizes promising uraniferous formations as "haystacks" and exploitable deposits as "needles." This, among other things, explains why prospecting for uranium can be an extremely expensive business. Although it can be comparatively easy with modern radiometric, magnetic, and geochemical instrumentation to find some trace showings, delineation of an exploitable ore body takes an extensive — and expensive — campaign of diamond drilling.

It should also be noted that final reserve tonnage, no matter how well established, will not in itself indicate how rapidly the resource can be extracted. Uranium developers are beginning to describe their prospects in terms of producibility, just as oilmen do — that is, how long will it take until a prospect is in production? Given certain cost and price parameters, how much uranium can be extracted in year one and in succeeding years of operation, bearing in mind the conservation of the resource and the company's contractual obligations?

These considerations have led to a great deal of controversy in the United States between uranium producers and developers and ERDA as to whether the nation's uranium resources are sufficient to meet future demand for nuclear fuel. This controversy will be discussed in the following chapter.

Finally, it should be emphasized that even after a deposit has been delineated, a very substantial amount of time must pass while a feasibility study is prepared and a plan adopted for the most effective means of exploiting the deposit. (Open-pit and underground mining are the two main options.) Strategies for removing the ore, which are consistent with the principle of maximizing output at the lowest possible cost, must be developed. Capital requirements for the enterprise must be raised. Then the actual removal of overburden or sinking of shafts begins; the ore-treating and -refining facilities are bid for and undertaken; and means of transportation are planned and built. The entire process, from the first strike by an exploration

FIGURE 2

Idealized Lead-Time Scale for Uranium Production

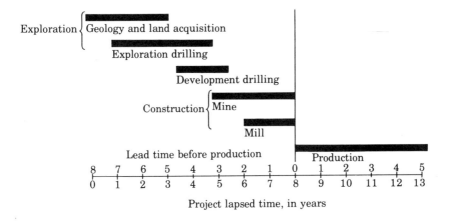

Project lapsed time, in years

Source: John Klemenic, "Analysis of Trends in Uranium Supply," unpublished paper given at ERDA Seminar, Grand Junction, Colorado, October, 1976.

team to the delivery of the uranium concentrate to market, typically takes seven to ten years. Figure 2 illustrates the time frame for bringing a uranium mine into production. While open-pit mines can be developed more rapidly, there is a declining trend in this type of operation, and no expansion in open-pit capacity is expected after 1982.

The Uranium Market, 1952-77

A brief history of the industry in Canada and the United States is useful in understanding why the price of uranium has suddenly risen and demand has skyrocketed. Chart 1 shows the pattern of price behaviour for uranium back to 1950.

The uranium-mining industry in North America mushroomed in the 1950s as the result of the world nuclear arms race and the concern by the U.S. Atomic Energy Commission (USAEC) to procure adequate supplies of uranium for its weapons program. Impelled by national security considerations, USAEC offered producers very favourable contracts which featured clauses permitting full amortization of their facilities over the life of a contract. Thus, having fulfilled his contract, a producer would have written off his mine and his mill and still have whatever remained of the reserve to exploit. Throughout the five-year period 1952-57, the average price paid by USAEC was over $11 per pound of oxide. Much of North America's uranium production still comes from such fully amortized facilities.

CHART 1

Uranium Prices in the United States, 1950-75[a]
(dollars per pound U_3O_8)

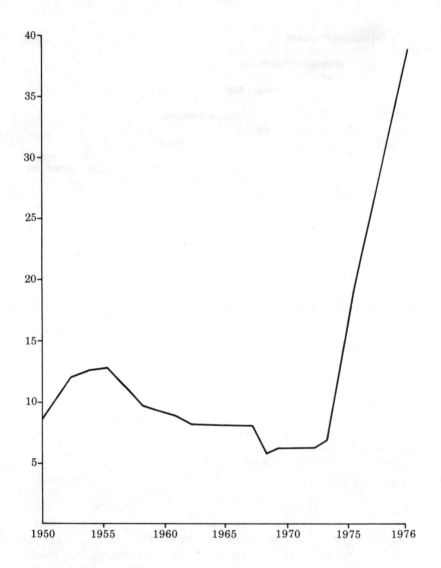

[a] Average annual spot prices.

Source: C. R. Lattanzi, "U_3O_8: An Analysis of Demand and Supply," unpublished
    report (Toronto: David S. Robertson & Associates, September, 1975), Figure 6
    for 1950-75 and updated for 1976 with figures from Nuclear Exchange Corpo-
    ration (NUEXCO).

From 1959 to 1962, U.S. mines produced an average of 18,000 tons of uranium per year; Canadian mines hit a peak of 16,000 tons in 1959. In that year, USAEC payments to Canadian producers totaled $330 million, making uranium Canada's most valuable mineral export.

USAEC soon realized it was getting more uranium than it needed and began a "stretch out" of existing contracts in order to avoid being stuck with an overwhelming stockpile. The price the United States paid for uranium also eroded, from $11 a pound in 1959 to $6.35 (and down to $4.00 in world markets) by 1969. Production sagged to about 11,000 tons per year in the United States and 4,000 tons in Canada. Many producers withdrew from the market; others found new markets as the demand for uranium as a nuclear fuel rather than as a weapons material increased. Rio Algom Mines Limited in Canada, for instance, signed a ten-year contract with the United Kingdom Atomic Energy Authority for several thousand tons a year as soon as the Canadian government authorized uranium exports for peaceful purposes in 1965. Sales were often made at prices less than production cost, let alone at prices that would justify new exploration. To allow the three major Canadian producers — Rio Algom Mines Limited, Eldorado Nuclear Limited, and Denison Mines Limited — to continue operating, in 1965 Canada established a uranium stockpile, making purchases at a bargain-basement $4.90 per pound of oxide. Canada had accumulated 10,000 tons of oxide by 1970 (and a further 3,200 tons in a special joint stockpile project with Denison Mines).

In 1972 two events of importance occurred. First, USAEC announced it would dispose of its stockpile of over 50,000 tons of uranium oxide on the commercial market. It adopted a complicated approach, known as "split tails," to minimize market disruption. (Essentially, this meant supplementing each consignment of private uranium supplied to enrichment plants with a certain proportion of uranium from government stockpiles.) However, the approach reduced uranium demand by about 20 percent during the 1972-75 period. The price slipped to $5.95 from $6.35 between January, 1969, and October, 1972 — a decline of about 25 percent in real dollars, allowing for then-current rates of inflation. Second, the U.S. government imposed an embargo on the import of foreign uranium for use in U.S. domestic nuclear facilities.

As analyzed by Nuclear Exchange Corporation (NUEXCO), the major U.S. private marketing organization, there were several factors simultaneously depressing the world market for nuclear fuel in the early 1970s. Government purchases under the stretch-out program were channeled into the commercial market, and the split-tails technique further contracted demand. The embargo on foreign feed convinced U.S. utilities that there was ample uranium abroad waiting to be contracted as soon as the embargo was lifted. Finally, the enrichment contracts offered by USAEC required only six months scheduling for forward deliveries for enrichment or, basically, an "on-demand" service. Because of all these factors, buyers hesitated to commit themselves to long-term contracts.[7]

One matter of mining economics cannot be overemphasized, since it runs directly counter to the traditional principles of economics. This is that higher prices for a mineable commodity do not necessarily result in an immediate increase of supply from existing mines. In fact, the effect can be the reverse — lower-grade ores can be processed economically, extending the life of existing mines but resulting in an actual decline of physical volume of refined production because the milling equipment in a mine is limited in tonnage capacity. This, for instance, happened in the South African gold industry during the sharp increase in the world price of gold in 1973. This too had an effect on the uranium supply. South African uranium production, which normally filled about 15 percent of world demand, was mainly a by-product of gold extraction and thus declined when leaner ores were mined.

During 1973-74 the cost of mining uranium increased steeply, not only because of the strong general inflationary pressures existing at the time, but because of the impact of more stringent environmental, health, and safety regulations. At the same time, USAEC ceased offering on-demand-type enrichment contracts and substituted long, fixed-commitment contracts for delivery up to eighteen years in the future. The uranium user was obligated to find a sufficient quantity of uranium to make up the necessary natural uranium feed.

Abruptly, what had been a buyers' market, dominated by spot selling and minimum inventory, became a sellers' market in which buyers were attempting to make the longest-term contracts with the minimum built-in price escalation. At the same time, U.S. producers, hit by termination of USAEC contracts, could not gear up quickly enough to meet the surge in demand.

It is important to note that all this happened before the Arab oil embargo was declared in November, 1973. To quote the NUEXCO report: "The Arab oil embargo served to drive home as nothing else before had, the importance to exporting countries of their energy resources. There were distinct reactions in Canada, South Africa, and Australia; the latter having already withdrawn from the market. New minerals policies were developed, and these countries became measurably more difficult to deal with. . . . The new high price for oil . . . provided a psychological basis for higher uranium oxide

---

[7] *Significant Events in the Uranium Market, 1969-76*, NUEXCO Special Report, January, 1977, p. 4.

prices. Sellers expected higher fuel prices and buyers became resigned to paying them."[8]

The disorganization of the uranium market that followed saw the price double in 1974, from $7.70 per pound to $15, and double again in 1975, to $35. Customers scurried for the largest amount of uranium for the longest terms they could manage. One major U.S. fuel fabricator, who had made extensive commitments to utility customers without having made covering purchases, announced in September, 1975, that it would be unable to deliver 33,000 tons of uranium oxide for which it had contracted, "due to commercial impracticability."

This caused a renewed scramble, as well as a variety of litigation, some of which is currently before the courts. It is worth noting, however, that in the opinion of NUEXCO the activities of a so-called "cartel" or "club" of foreign producers — of which more than one Canadian company has been alleged to be a member — "had little or no effect on uranium prices. . . . It was the governments of these countries which clearly were the dominant parties, often determining uranium marketing policies." And "the prices reportedly established by the 'cartel' at its periodic gatherings were . . . below those then prevailing in the domestic marketplace. The cartel was, in fact, in a position of trying to catch up with the domestic market."[9]

Prospects for Canadian Supply

The current dissension and disorganization in the U.S. uranium market are clearly having an effect on Canada. Unlike the United States, Canada is in no immediate danger of a shortfall in nuclear fuel requirements on the basis of present resource estimates and planned installation of nuclear power capacity. This is so even with the federal government's policy enunciation that domestic uranium supplies sufficient for all planned nuclear reactors for thirty years at an 80 percent load factor (or a total of 81,000 tons of oxide) must be set aside. Chapter 4 focuses on the delineation of known Canadian uranium resources and discusses the political, technological, and economic factors governing their expansion and producibility to the year 2000.

The current situation can be summed up in the words of a report by Energy, Mines and Resources Canada: "Canadian uranium producers have contractual export commitments for about 110,000 short tons of uranium oxide. . . . Over and above these commitments and their domestic allocations Canadian producers will still have almost 50 percent of their adjusted resources uncommitted to meet

---

[8] *Ibid.*, p. 6.
[9] *Ibid.*, p. 7.

future export or domestic needs."[10] Most existing commitments are to Japanese and European customers.

Canada, then, looks to a future where it will continue to export uranium in the world market. Once the United States is firmly back in the market for imported uranium, it will become an important factor in this market. (By 1980, U.S. utilities will be able to import up to 50 percent of their uranium requirements for nuclear fuel.)

The major factor in determining the extent to which U.S. requirements will be met from imports will be the price and the producibility of uranium from domestic sources and the extent to which these can be augmented by further discoveries. The following chapter looks at the domestic uranium picture in the United States.

---

[10] Energy, Mines and Resources Canada, *1975 Assessment of Canada's Uranium Supply and Demand* (Ottawa: Supply and Services Canada, 1976), p. 6.

3

The Uncertain Picture of U.S. Uranium Resources

The purpose of this chapter is to look at estimates of known uranium resources in the United States and to examine the probable curve of uranium supplies available annually from these resources and how these can be anticipated to match the most likely levels of demand for nuclear fuel to the year 2000, bearing in mind the uncertainty of both resource estimates and demand forecasts.

In projecting the future supply of any mineable mineral over a period as long as twenty-three years, there are two sets of data to be taken into account: (a) the quantity and the quality of ore known to be in the ground in deposits already discovered and delineated and (b) estimates, based on geological inference, of the rate of discovery of new deposits and of their extent and richness. An implicit variable affecting both sets of numbers is the market price expected for the commodity. If the market price exceeds the cost of production of a given deposit, exploitation of the ore is economically viable. Obviously, the higher the price, the greater the measurable forward supply of the commodity.

For uranium, the first set of variables is known as "reasonably assured resources," or RAR, while the second is called "estimated additional resources," or EAR.[1] Cost of production is usually given in U.S. dollars per pound of uranium oxide (U_3O_8). The recent escalation of uranium prices has enormously expanded the share of the world's resources that could be economically exploited, although this has, in part, been limited by concurrent increases in costs of extraction. As recently as 1975, resource estimates were made in terms of uranium available at an estimated cost of production of $8; today $15 and $30 costs are the commonest measuring sticks.

It is worth noting that an important variable affecting the cost of most mineable commodities to the final consumer is missing from

---

[1] These formulations were developed jointly by the Nuclear Energy Agency of the OECD and the United Nations' International Atomic Energy Agency, or NEA/IAEA for short.

the uranium equation: transportation costs, for a commodity worth up to $80,000 a ton in the marketplace, can be virtually disregarded once the ore has been milled and processed into concentrate.

At the same time that higher prices can be expected to increase projections of supply of exploitable uranium in any given area, they can also be expected to contract total demand. Uranium demand, however, is relatively price-inelastic, since the cost of enrichment, fuel fabrication, and construction of nuclear power plants is many times greater than the cost of natural uranium. Moreover, nuclear power plants cannot be converted to another fuel — the way, for example, an oil-burning plant might be converted to coal or gas — should the cost of the fuel suddenly increase.

Nor can uranium supply be said to be price-elastic, since it is governed by long-term contracts with price-adjustment clauses, usually annual. However, in the long term, uranium exploration and development are highly price-elastic. One explanation for the rapid rise in the price of uranium in the past four years is that the previously depressed price had discouraged the finding and development of new deposits and impelled the closing of marginal deposits.

ERDA, the primary U.S. authority for making estimates of national uranium reserves, took over this responsibility from the USAEC in 1974. It categorizes U.S. uranium resources as "reserves" or as "probable," "possible," or "speculative" resources. These are further classified into two cost categories — uranium available at up to $15 a pound of U_3O_8 and uranium available at costs of between $15 and $30 a pound.[2] The agency admits that "estimates of reserves in the $30 category are less reliable because of lack of mining experience with low grade ore."[3] ERDA defines its resource categories as follows:

- Reserves are uranium deposits that have been drilled and sampled. The amount of uranium that could be produced is estimated by engineering, geologic, and economic appraisal techniques.
- Probable resources are those believed present in known productive uranium districts, as extensions of known deposits, or in undiscovered deposits within known geological trends.
- Possible resources are those estimated to occur in partly defined deposits in formations not previously productive or in a geological area not previously productive.
- Speculative resources are those located outside known uranium districts.

---

[2] Costs are defined by ERDA to include normal operating and capital costs that have not been incurred at the time the reserves estimate is made. Significantly, the costs associated with exploration, land acquisition, and development are excluded from this definition, thereby rendering any profitability analysis of little value.

[3] Energy Research and Development Administration, *National Uranium Resources Evaluation*, Preliminary Report, June, 1976, p. 10.

As of January 1, 1977, total U.S. uranium reserves producible at a forward "cost" of $30 a pound were estimated by ERDA to total 680,000 tons U_3O_8, with another 140,000 tons expected to be recoverable over the next twenty-five years from phosphate and copper production. An even larger amount — 1,090,000 tons — was classified as a probable resource, with 1,120,000 tons as possible, and 480,000 tons as speculative.[4] All established reserves are in the western United States, as are most deposits under other resource classifications.

Resource estimates are revised each year. In commenting on changes from its previous estimates, the most recent ERDA report states: "The changes in potential resources estimates in the $30 cost category during 1976 amount to a slight increase in the probable potential resource class, and decreases in the possible and speculative classes."[5] During 1976 about 100,000 tons of reserves were added to the $30 cost category, but 46,000 tons were removed from that category because of the increased costs of exploiting them, and 14,000 tons were mined. Thus, only a net 40,000 tons were added to proven resources in 1976 at the $30 cost level.

Interestingly, in a recent report ERDA made a preliminary estimate of reserves and resources in the $50-a-pound cost category for the first time. The report says that these "are preliminary and less reliable than . . . estimates of lower cost reserves. . . . Not all of this reserve increment will actually become available at these costs."[6] ERDA estimates that an additional 160,000 tons of uranium oxide will become available at the $50-per-pound limit on the cost of extraction. Probable and possible resource estimates are increased about 25 percent each by the inclusion of $30-50-per-pound resources. This indicates an important fact: increased prices for a resource do not necessarily bring about a corresponding increase in supply if the resource base itself is limited.

The basic assumption ERDA makes in estimating resources is that an area being appraised can be compared with a known thoroughly explored area with respect to size and key physical and geological characteristics. A mine realization factor (T) is based on past production plus ore reserves of the control area. The National Uranium Resources Evaluation (NURE) report offers this hypothetical example of the procedure for potential resource estimation. The magnitude of potential resources in an area is determined by the formula

$$\text{Potential} = N \times F \times U \times T$$

where N is the extent of favourable ground in square, linear, or cubic miles; F is the "favourability factor" from a comparison of the

---

[4] Energy Research and Development Administration, *Statistical Data of the Uranium Industry* (Grand Junction, Colorado, 1977).

[5] *Ibid.*, p. 43.

[6] *Ibid.*, p. 21.

characteristics of the area compared to the control area; U is the percentage of the area that has not yet been explored; and T is the mine realization factor already defined. For example, a certain area in a type of formation called a "roll front" in Wyoming indicates that an area extending thirty-five miles is potentially favourable for uranium. Comparison with the control area indicates only a 40 percent favourability factor. Only 30 percent of the area has been explored, making $U = 70$ percent. The control area exhibits a reserve plus production of 2,000 tons of uranium oxide per mile of front. The formula therefore indicates that the potential resource is 35 x .40 x .70 x 2,000, or 19,600 tons of uranium oxide. ERDA admits that "an appropriate statistical basis for establishing confidence limits" for the potential resource estimates does not yet exist.

In looking forward from the data presented in the NURE report, the authors make the following conclusions:

- Guarded optimism permits the conclusion that significant increases in present resource estimates will result from current and future investigations.
- Conventional sandstone-type resources may well be further expanded in and near producing districts as well as in nonproducing areas.
- Future discoveries may include deposits of types different from the sandstone-type ores that form the bulk of known resources in the United States. There is a reasonable opportunity for discovery of deposits similar to those now known in Australia, Canada, and South Africa. However, only limited parts of the United States may be geologically favourable for such deposits.
- Prompt and vigorous exploration and development will be required to make new discoveries and to convert potential resources to reserves at a rate adequate to support projected nuclear power expansion.[7]

There is concern, however, on the part of some U.S. producers that ERDA's "guarded optimism" cannot be readily substantiated. As will be seen later when the Canadian classification scheme is examined, the Canadian approach is much more conservative than that used by ERDA, as are the internationally accepted NEA-IAEA classifications.

Productive Capability Is Crucial

Regardless of the actual extent of U.S. uranium resources in various cost categories, domestic supplies of nuclear fuel materials in the 1977-2000 period will depend primarily on the productive capacity of the U.S. uranium industry. The pace of resource de-

---

[7] Energy Research and Development Administration, *National Uranium Resources Evaluation, op. cit.*, pp. 10-15.

velopment will be limited by the price incentives for uranium exploration, by the availability and cost of mining personnel and equipment, and, at the end of the supply chain, by the pace of development of processing and enrichment facilities.

CHART 2

Estimated Uranium Production Capability in the United States to 1990
(tons U₃O₈ in concentrate)

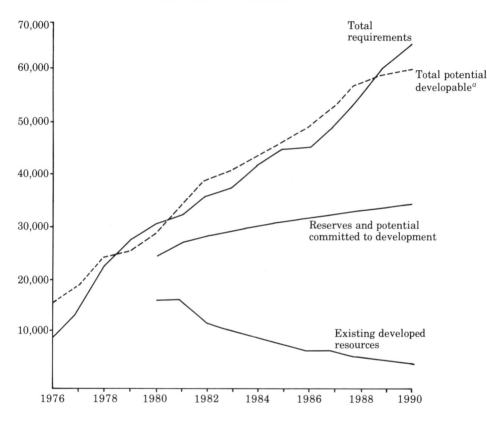

^{a} For the period 1976-79, total potential developable is based on industry production
plans.
Source: Energy Research and Development Administration, *National Uranium Resources Evaluation*, Preliminary Report, June, 1976.

ERDA has at times been criticized for what many consider to be
the agency's overly optimistic view of future supply generation.
Chart 2 summarizes ERDA's estimation of the production capacity of
the uranium industry and compares this capability with anticipated
domestic requirements. ERDA anticipates that the combination of

known and potential resources will more than meet future requirements to 1988. The margin of surplus production, though, is a thin
one. ERDA estimates that production of U_3O_8 could rise from 16,000
to 61,000 tons per year in the fifteen-year period. Only half this production, however, would come from established reserves; the rest
would have to be discovered. A minimum expenditure of $17 billion
(constant 1976 dollars) would be required to accomplish this, plus
another $3 billion in exploration costs to establish an eight-year
forward reserve. The manpower pool of underground miners would
have to expand at a rate of 12 percent per year.

A major uncertainty in this forecast is whether ERDA has ade-
quately allowed for the effect of lower-grade ore on fixed milling
capacity, which would reduce production totals. U.S. mills were reported to have operated at two-thirds of capacity in 1975 because
they were rated at 18,000 tons of concentrate production and produced only 12,300 tons. With average U.S. ore grade having slipped
from 0.23 percent to 0.16 percent in the past ten years, U.S. mills
probably, in fact, operated at near capacity. The situation may now
be even worse because the current high prices on the spot market
are reported to be bringing to the mills low-grade ore down to 0.05
percent uranium. It seems a rather paradoxical economic effect that,
in the short run, continuing high prices may well depress U.S. (and
world) uranium production temporarily.

This scenario has come under fire from within the industry for
two quite different reasons.[8] One group believes that the U.S.
uranium-producing industry would be extremely hard-pressed to
meet these demands, especially now that a plutonium-recycling system has been indefinitely postponed. A second group of producers is
concerned that such forecasts of excess supply in the 1980s may
prompt the managements of producing companies, especially those
who remember the lean years in the 1960s, to cut back on exploration and development.

Typical of the skepticism is an analysis by David S. Robertson &
Associates, which concludes that potential supply from known reserves is insufficient to satisfy projected Western world demand
beyond 1979:

> If the United States is to maintain self-sufficiency it alone will require a
> discovery rate of about 75,000 to 100,000 tons of uranium oxide a
> year.... Over the last 25 years, the average rate of discovery of low cost
> reserves in the United States has been about 20,000 tons of uranium
> oxide per year.... No truly new uranium producing district has been

---

[8] When the original USAEC estimate of 740,000 tons of uranium available at a cost
of $30 was made in 1974, it was subjected to the scrutiny of thirty-six geologists in
various resource companies. Using the same evidence, their average estimate was
450,000 tons. (See National Science Foundation, *Papers of the Committee on Mineral Resources and the Environment (COMRATE) Conference*, Albuquerque, N.M.
[Washington, D.C., 1975].)

discovered in the United States for more than 15 years. Future search for new reserves will necessarily become more "wildcat" in nature, and it will be extremely difficult to maintain the discovery rates of previous years. . . . It is not intended to imply that there is any absolute shortage of uranium, rather it is suggested that the exploration effort must be accelerated and that production must be commenced from less favourable deposits as these are discovered. These factors imply continuing increases in the real price of uranium.[9]

There is also some skepticism about the 140,000 tons of uranium supposed to be recovered in the next twenty-five years as a by-product of phosphate and copper production. In fact, John Klemenic of ERDA, in his supply analysis of October, 1976, says: "Uranium recovery from phosphate is risky because the investment is dependent on the fertilizer market and the solvent used for uranium extraction could interfere with the process. Uranium recovery as a by-product of copper operations is expected to contribute only slight amounts to our overall future supply."[10] While further process development has enhanced optimism about phosphate recovery, by-product recovery is a poor hedge against uranium scarcity.

In commenting on ERDA's earlier 1975 reserves projection, Canadian geologist D. S. Robertson noted that "reserves of lower cost categories are reasonably assured and are estimated in much the same way as for other commodities. In spite of this, much of the reserve is estimated too loosely to be acceptable to the U.S. Securities and Exchange Commission" as adequate evidence of a producible asset required for a stock issue to the public. Further, the higher-cost ($15-30) reserves "cannot be relied upon as sources of supply as price moves to higher levels."[11]

In 1974, ERDA predicted the cumulative uranium requirements of the United States from 1975 to 1983 to be 222,000 tons. While this has generally been accepted as sufficient, Robertson makes two salient points. First, suppose that the Canadian practice of protecting a thirty-year supply for reactors in use or under construction were instituted in the United States, then the United States would need 600,000 tons of reserves, or nearly three times ERDA's estimates. Second, there is a critical difference between the concept of reserves and that of productive capability. For instance, exploitation of lower-grade ore requires a more-than-proportionate increase in the capacity of the mills. His remarks on the "resource numbers game" bear consideration:

[9] C. R. Lattanzi, "U3O8: An Analysis of Demand and Supply," unpublished report (Toronto: David S. Robertson & Associates, September, 1975), pp. 10-12. The 1976 net addition to proven reserves is reported as 40,000 tons at a cost of under $30 per pound.
[10] John Klemenic, "Analysis of Trends in Uranium Supply," unpublished paper given at ERDA Seminar, Grand Junction, Colorado, October, 1976.
[11] D. S. Robertson, "Power Through the Next 25 Years," unpublished paper presented at American Society of Mechanical Engineers Conference, September, 1975.

One might have thought that the sharp reduction of North American oil and gas resource estimates of the last few years would have created some feeling of caution in development of resource figures which have much less secure geological or statistical bases.

That the producer industry does not accept this "resources is real" point of view is suggested by its production plans which are based solely on reserves, and by its refusal to contract for sales of material which it cannot measure as ore in the ground.

Resource numbers are useful, he suggests, only to guide geological judgment as to whether a particular area warrants exploration or not.

Robertson concludes:

The anticipated demand for uranium in the United States cannot be satisfied by production from known domestic reserves beyond the next few years. . . . Our studies of the exploration and development process do not make us optimistic about achieving the production levels required through the next ten years. Shortfalls against near term demand should be anticipated.

U.S. geologist John Gabelman complains that "uranium explorationists [in the United States] have become relatively complacent in applying the exploration technology of the comparatively easily recognizeable sandstone uranium deposits of the Colorado Region."[12] He points out that current technology used in exploration depends on reserve data derived only from penetration of the subsurface. Yet industry has not been disposed to perform or subsidize further the geologic studies. Gabelman makes an appeal to industry to do more investigation of untouched low-grade deposits, instead of visualizing exploration targets in terms of known resources. He comments that during the lean "stretch-out" period, when the price of uranium declined to $6.90, producers "picked the eyes" out of deposits. The recognition of an impending shortage has allowed extraction of marginal, low-grade ores. However, because of earlier high grading, "the additional reserves made available by extending ore body margins proved relatively insignificant."[13]

However, the "unconventional" uranium deposits that Gabelman suggests the industry should examine are high-cost sources, such as monazite placers,[14] Florida phosphate rock, and uranium-bearing coals and lignites, along with carbonaceous shale. The monazite placers may be significant later, when thorium values become important, but U.S. deposits in South Carolina, Georgia, and Idaho "are volumetrically insignificant." In addition, there are hopes held for by-product extraction of uranium from otherwise valuable phosphate rock. There are also sources such as the Chattanooga shales, with a uranium content of about two ounces per ton, as a likely

---

[12] John Gabelman, "Expectations from Uranium Exploration," *AAPG Bulletin*, November, 1976, p. 1993.

[13] *Loc. cit.*

[14] Stream-bed deposits of monazite, a mineral containing thorium and minute quantities of uranium.

prospect. Some marginal conventional uranium ore as low-grade as this is already being milled in the United States. The main problems in exploitation, says Gabelman, are "economic release of uranium from the carbon and the environmental problems of large open pit mines."[15]

The natural reluctance of the industry to initiate exploration towards higher-cost reserves is admitted by Gabelman. This "derives from the constant threat of discovery of new low-cost resources. . . . Once locked into high cost unconventional resources, an operation could not compete with ample supplies of conventional resources."[16]

Nor does Gabelman appreciate the effect of capital-cost escalations on current large industrial projects. His estimate of $21-42 a pound for uranium from shale, for instance, is based on a flat 40 percent escalation factor from cost figures developed by the USAEC in the mid-1960s. Current estimates show that a threefold escalation for large projects has been more usual in the past decade. This would put the realistic cost of extracting uranium from shale in the $60-120 range — practical only in the event of a drastic world shortage of the resource.

In contrast to these pessimistic views is the report of a prestigious energy policy study group chaired by Spurgeon M. Keeny, Jr., sponsored by the Ford Foundation and administered by Mitre Corporation.[17] The report's analysis of uranium supply, "based on typical ERDA planning scenarios, indicates that all predicted demand levels for LWRs (light water reactors) could be accommodated with a reasonable expansion of present reserves at prices not exceeding $40/lb. (1975 dollars) for the balance of this century, and that uranium resources will probably be adequate well into the next century."[18] Nevertheless, it recommends intensified exploration efforts.

In addition, a recent report by TRW Systems Inc. for the State of California, entitled "Assessment of Electrical Generation Methods," suggests that "known reserves and probable potential resources of U_3O_8 should be sufficient to fill projected needs until the 1990s."[19] After the early 1990s some of the alternatives the report suggests for meeting demand requirements include the discovery of new reserves, the use of foreign imports, the use of lower-grade ores,

[15] Gabelman, op. cit., p. 1995.
[16] Ibid., p. 1996.
[17] Spurgeon M. Keeny, Jr., et al., Nuclear Power Issues and Choices (Cambridge, Mass.: Ballinger Publishing Company, 1977).
[18] Ibid., p. 74.
[19] California Electricity Generating Methods Assessment, prepared for the State of California by TRW Systems Inc., Redondo Beach, California, January, 1977, pp. 2-31.

the use of plutonium recycling, and the use of more efficient reactors such as the high-temperature, gas-cooled reactor and the CANDU.[20] However, the authors of the report admit that "a detailed review of these studies [of uranium supply and demand] was not made due to time limitations. As an item for additional research, we recommended that. . . these studies be analyzed as a means for developing a good forecast of the future market for uranium." In short, the authors' optimism appears to be based on an uncritical acceptance of the NURE preliminary study. Also, plutonium recycling can no longer be considered a near-term alternative.

Uranium Supply: Outlook for Expansion

Both optimists and pessimists concur that it is urgent that large, secure supplies of uranium be developed and produced quickly in the United States. To achieve this, the scale of uranium exploration would have to be increased, many large finds would have to be made, and development would have to follow the pattern projected in the NURE report. While producibility will still present a bottleneck, there are both legislative and technological expedients that can be applied.

In the United States, underground mining will provide the major expansion in production. Most high-grade deposits recoverable by open-pit methods have already been developed. Cut-off grades for open-pit mines are usually lower than for underground mines because they have lower marginal production costs. A sharp drop in grade is expected in open-pit mining during the 1978-79 period as established producers lower cut-off grades and new, low-grade, open-pit mines are started. Chart 3 indicates the relative growth in importance of underground mining anticipated by ERDA in the period to 1990.

Underground mining is much more labour-intensive than open-pit mining, so labour supply is likely to be a problem. New schools to train miners have been inaugurated, but the shortage of skilled miners is likely to persist. Approximately 2,000 underground miners are working today, and according to the NURE report, projections for 1990 indicate that more than 10,000 will be required in that year. The pool of skilled underground miners needs to expand at a continually compounded rate of at least 12 percent a year. Because of retirement and job-transfer factors, an average of 800 new miners need to be trained each year of the fifteen-year period.[21]

---

[20] The high-temperature, gas-cooled reactor has been written off by ERDA as not viable until after 1995. Earlier hopes for this new system have faded because of operational difficulties with prototypes such as the Peach Bottom station in the United States.

[21] ERDA, *National Uranium Resources Evaluation, op. cit.*, p. 16.

CHART 3

**Estimated U.S. Uranium-Ore-Production
Capability, by Type of Mine, 1976-90**[a]
(thousand tons per day)

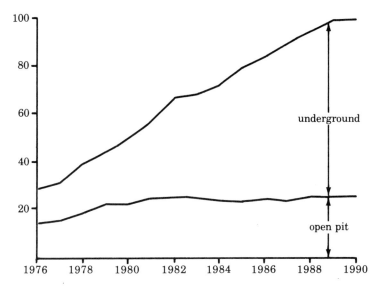

[a] Estimates refer to ore that could be mined and milled at $15 per pound of U_3O_8 as of January 1, 1976.

Source: John Klemenic, "Analysis of Trends in Uranium Supply," unpublished paper given at ERDA Seminar, Grand Junction, Colorado, October, 1976.

A brief examination of Canadian experience in expanding underground mining activity is instructive. In Canada, underground mining has always been the dominant method employed to extract uranium. At present there is a labour shortage in mining because immigration from areas that have traditionally supplied recruits to the mining industry has been declining, and it is difficult to attract native Canadians into mining. Moreover, many uranium mines are in remote, uninhabited northern areas, and labour turnover in such mining-camp situations typically runs from 100 to 200 percent a year, a situation offering little encouragement for attempts to upgrade the technical skills of miners.

Efforts are being made to alleviate this situation. "The traditional spartan concept of a miner's life must change," says N. M. Ediger, president of Eldorado Nuclear Limited. He suggests "innovations such as commuting to the mine site, employment of working couples, hiring of more women for production jobs, and the building of more elaborate infrastructures."[22] Gulf Minerals, at Rabbit Lake, Saskatchewan, for instance, has a program that provides aerial commuting services between the mine site and centres of population. Workers, housed in a motel-like camp, work alternate weeks; as a result, the program has cut labour force turnover dramatically.

There are other impediments to a rapid buildup of a pool of skilled uranium-mining labour. First, safety considerations, particularly those in regard to radiation, have acted as a deterrent to attracting new uranium miners into the labour force. Second, expertise in the mining of other metals, because of the unique characteristics of uranium deposits, is not easily transferable to uranium mining. This limits the potential entry of other miners into the uranium labour force, even during times of depressed conditions in base-metals markets, when such additional labour may be widely available.

Another way to get around the labour shortage problem would be greater use of solution mining, which allows greater production from underground deposits with a smaller work force. Solution mining involves leaching uranium deposits out of underground rock with either acid solution or bacterial action. Uranium-rich solutions from either type of leaching are stripped at the surface by an ion exchange column.[23] While solution mining is less labour-intensive than conventional underground mining, it is economic only when applied to certain types of deposits, or when used to recover residual ore values from properties that have already been exploited by conventional techniques.

The increasing interest in solution mining of uranium is largely due to technological advances in methods of *in situ* leaching.[24] The successful application of this technology is indicated by the number of projects presently under way. In the United States there are three new solution-mining projects going into operation in Texas: U.S. Steel and Niagara Mohawk at George West, Mobil Oil at Bruni, and Wyoming Minerals at Moglia. Several other companies are planning solution-mining projects: Westinghouse, Nuclear Dynamics/Bethlehem Steel, Power Resources, and Intercontinental Energy, for instance. "The growth of the solution mining industry is regarded as much more certain than that of by-product recovery," report the NURE authors.[25] While 1976 uranium production from solution mines in the United States was only 300 tons, production from the three properties is projected to reach 4,000 tons annually by 1985.

[22] N. M. Ediger, "Canadian Uranium: The New Economics," address to the International Conference on Uranium, Geneva, September 14, 1976.
[23] The Stanrock Mine in the Elliot Lake region of Canada produced 25,000 pounds of oxide a month in the mid-1960s by means of bacterial leaching.
[24] See, for instance, NUEXCO Report No. 101, p. 1.5.
[25] ERDA, *National Uranium Resources Evaluation, op. cit.*, p. 119.

(This will still provide less than 10 percent of U.S. requirements, however.)

Should uranium prospectors be lucky, and mine development find adequate capital, equipment, and labour, uranium supply might again be in balance with demand, and uranium prices could remain stable or even decline.

Limited Enrichment Capacity

Another constraint on uranium-supply generation in the United States is the situation of ERDA's three gaseous diffusion plants, which separate natural uranium into enriched (3 percent U-235) and depleted streams. The total capacity of these gigantic plants, built between World War II and the late 1950s, is already strained, one reason being the foreign commitments undertaken by the United States in backing the drive of U.S. industry to sell BWR and PWR technology abroad. About one-third of enrichment capacity is dedicated to contracts to foreign users, supplying a total of 115,000 megawatts of offshore nuclear electric capacity, while U.S. utility commitments total 208,000 megawatts capacity. In December, 1976, for instance, nearly 50 percent of "separative work" that ERDA performed in its enrichment plants (some $41 million out of a total of $85 million of enrichment production) was for foreign customers, principally for the Euratom group and Japan.

"Separative work units" (SWU) is a technical term difficult to define in lay terms; basically the number of SWU defines the separation capacity of the enrichment plant. A higher level of SWU permits a plant to increase the amount of enriched uranium produced from a given volume of natural uranium. Put differently, a fixed amount of SWU means that more natural uranium fuel is required to extract a greater quantity of fuel-grade enriched uranium. Efficiency is then measured, in rough terms, by the level of U-235 retained in the "tails" or depleted material. Currently, ERDA supply contracts call for a tails level of 0.20 percent U-235; however, U.S. plants are not able to meet this specification and still produce the desired output quantity and are actually operating at less efficient levels of 0.25 and, in some cases, even higher. This difference between "transaction" and "operating" tails increases the amount of unenriched uranium feed required.

Closing the Fuel Cycle

The major change in the outlook for U.S. uranium requirements stems from President Carter's announcement in April, 1977, that his Administration was foreclosing the option of "closing the fuel cycle."

As described in Chapter 2, it is possible to reprocess nuclear fuel to extract plutonium and to use it either as fuel for a fast reactor or to add to enriched or natural uranium fuel (which is then characterized as "mixed-oxide" fuel). Plans for a fuel-reprocessing plant in the United States had already been stalled for several years. The first plant at Barnwell, South Carolina, owned by Allied-General Nuclear Services, is still incomplete, and the specifications for a waste-control system have not even been formulated yet. It is not now likely to be commissioned in the near future. The reprocessing decision means that steady-state uranium requirements for projected nuclear power capacity will be about 40 percent greater in terms of fissile content by the early 1990s. This does not include initial fuel commitments for new reactors.

A decision to delay nuclear fuel reprocessing indefinitely is recommended by the Ford-Mitre Report, on the basis that there is no economic proof that it could substantially reduce the price of nuclear-generated electric power before 2000 despite the admission that full reprocessing would raise U.S. uranium requirements by 300,000 tons in the 1977-2000 period. In their assessment, "plutonium could do little to improve nuclear fuel economics or assurance here or abroad. This conclusion rests on our analysis of uranium supply, the economics of plutonium recycle in current reactors, and the prospects of breeder reactors."[26]

The concluding paragraph in the report's treatment of uranium supply suggests that its authors are implicitly downgrading the importance of domestic self-sufficiency in uranium, in pursuit of the objective of achieving international agreement to slow the drive towards closing the nuclear fuel cycle, until some solutions to the security and the environmental problems of spent-fuel reprocessing can be evolved.

> Foreign sources of supply are large and growing. The door has been opened to imports, and much larger imports may be desirable. . . . The slow schedule for full removal of import restrictions could be revised in the light of these considerations.[27]

Whether other developed countries will be willing to suspend their own programs to close the fuel cycle is still a moot point. While initial reaction to Carter's policy statement by nuclear authorities in Europe and Japan was chilly, a seven-nation study — the International Nuclear Fuel Cycle Evaluation Program — has been agreed to by Britain, Canada, France, Italy, Japan, West Germany, and the United States. Current indications are that Britain, France, and Germany plan to proceed with expanded oxide-reprocessing capability regardless of the U.S. position on the subject. INFCEP will probably have no impact on the decision of these countries to move ahead with reprocessing capability. Even if the United States goes it alone, the extra 300,000 tons of uranium required by the year 2000 will have a major impact on the world supply picture.

---

[26] Keeny, *op. cit.*, p. 29.
[27] *Ibid.*, p. 94.

One solution is to increase enrichment capacity. In addition to ERDA's Portsmouth, Ohio, plant, Congress has already approved increasing total U.S. separatory capacity by about 30 percent. Even without the recycling of fuel, this would allow the diffusion plants to go back to a 0.20 percent tails assay level. However, no funding has yet been authorized for the plant, which will probably cost close to $4 billion, nor has any date for commencing construction been announced.

According to recent Carter energy policy, the United States is to expand its enrichment capacity. Carter's statement also indicated that the United States would guarantee enrichment facilities to all nations accepting a non-proliferation agreement. However, President Carter's agreement to expand enrichment technology was conditional upon substituting ultra-centrifuge separation for the established diffusion-plant technology on the grounds that it is more economical of electricity. The centrifuge technology, developed by Urenco in Europe, has never been applied to as large a plant as is required in the United States. While there appears to be no problem in funding the Portsmouth expansion, it is likely that problems of scale-up will prevent full planned production until the mid-1980s. However, the modular nature of the technology permits commercial-scale facilities to have considerably smaller capacities than diffusion plants.

There have been some moves by private enterprise to get into the enrichment business in the United States. Considering the difficulties of private fuel-reprocessing projects, it is not considered likely that this will affect events to 1985.

The Outlook for Uranium Demand

Demand for uranium, assuming no significant increase in weapons production, is primarily determined by nuclear power production. Future escalation in uranium demand can therefore be tied to plans for nuclear generation capacity. ERDA estimates of nuclear power capacity have been severely scaled down since 1975, a move that seems to have gone unnoticed by many uranium supply forecasters outside the United States. This downward assessment seems a little surprising, since U.S. power installations are performing quite well at this point. They generated over 201 million megawatt hours in 1976, an increase of 11 percent over 1975, and five new nuclear power stations were commissioned in 1976.[28]

In its 1975 forecast, ERDA projected that 205,000 megawatts of installed nuclear capacity would be in place by 1985.[29] A forecast released in 1976 cuts back expectations to a range of 127,000-160,000

---

[28] Megawatt hours measure the total quantity of electricity generated over time.
[29] Megawatt capacity measures the maximum instantaneous output of electricity from electrical-power plants.

megawatts, with a mid-range estimate of 145,000 megawatts. This mid-range forecast is predicted on the assumption that total energy growth to 1985 will average 3.1 percent yearly (the historical average is 3.7 percent).

As a consequence of the newer, lower forecasts, uranium requirements to 1985 and beyond have been revised downward by ERDA. Annual estimates for 1985 range from 32,000 to 45,000 tons, with a most recent mid-range estimate of 39,900 tons.

ERDA projections were based on the following assumptions regarding the development of alternative nuclear power systems: the high-temperature, gas-cooled reactor was not assumed to re-enter the U.S. reactor market until 1995, thereby having little impact on uranium demand to 2000; and fast-breeder reactors were assumed to begin commercial operation in the year 1995. This alternative, as stated earlier, has now been ruled out. It was also assumed that the characteristics of light-water reactors, currently in use in the United States, would not alter markedly over the forecast period. A 70-percent-capacity utilization factor is assumed, except for reactors in their startup and obsolescence phases. (This utilization factor is higher than current U.S. experience, with the exception of New England.)

TABLE 1

U.S. Uranium Supply and Demand, 1977-85
(short tons U_3O_8)

Year	Domestic Contracts	Imports	Total	Requirements	Theoretical Surplus (+) or Deficit (−) of Supply
1977	15,800	4,000	19,800	12,300	+6,500
1978	17,900	2,900	20,800	19,800	+1,000
1979	18,400	3,300	21,700	24,400	−2,700
1980	20,400	4,200	24,600	28,600	−4,000
1981	19,000	4,300	23,300	32,300	−9,000
1982	19,200	4,100	13,300	36,100	−12,100
1983	15,000	4,100	19,100	35,500	−16,400
1984	13,000	3,800	16,800	41,300	−24,500
1985	11,500	3,500	15,000	39,900	−24,900

Note: Figures for domestic and foreign supply and for enrichment feed requirements are based on existing contracts only. Surplus and deficit figures are therefore only theoretical. New supply contracts may be called to meet enrichment-feed obligations, and enrichment requirements may be slipped or altered.

Source: Energy Research and Development Administration, *Statistical Data of the Uranium Industry* (Grand Junction, Colorado, 1977).

Table 1 shows ERDA estimates of annual requirements for the years 1977 to 1985 based on existing enrichment contracts for nuclear reactors scheduled for startup up to that year. Uranium demand for 1985 is rather inflexible. It is constrained on the upside by lead time considerations and on the downside by DOE fixed-commitment enrichment contracts. ERDA statistics for 1977 contained no forecast of uranium requirements past 1985. In the *National Uranium Resources Evaluation* preliminary report published by ERDA in 1976, a forecast of uranium requirements to 2000 gave figures of 39,000 tons annual requirements by 1985 and 90,000 tons by the year 2000.

The forecast is based on 0.20 percent transaction tails level of enrichment to 1980 and 0.25 percent thereafter. While, as has been pointed out, differences in tails assay may affect requirements substantially, this is a cumulative effect and would not be expected to make a substantial difference before 1985. In a paper given at Geneva in September, 1976,[30] E. J. Hanrahan, Director of Analysis for ERDA, projected that, with no reprocessing, uranium demands would be 10-20 percent higher during the period to 2000. A paper delivered by John Klemenic, ERDA's Director of Supply Analysis, at a seminar at Grand Junction, Colorado,[31] forecast annual uranium requirements of 46,000 tons by 1985 and 102,000 tons by 2000. This variation in three forecasts generated within the same organization within the same twelve-month period suggests a high degree of uncertainty in the uranium supply outlook.

The movement of domestic and international price levels for uranium concentrate will have a substantial effect upon the generation of long-term supply from both domestic and foreign sources. There is now a marked discrepancy between the average price for existing contracts (still around the $15-a-pound level) and the price for contracts now being negotiated.[32] These are within 90-100 percent of the spot price in the world market, which rose steeply to $41.00 per pound late in 1976 and closed at $43.20 in 1977, registering only a $2.20 per pound escalation in that year. Based on financial considerations alone (that is, the expected trend of the U.S. prime rate of interest), NUEXCO predicts a current-dollar cost of U_3O_8 of between $60 and $75 per pound by the end of 1982. The uranium market is said by analysts to be "no longer hectic." While at present production-cost levels there seems no reason for any rapid

---

[30] E. J. Hanrahan, "World Requirements and Supply of Uranium," unpublished paper presented at the Atomic Industrial Forum International Conference on Uranium, Geneva, September 14, 1976, p. 19.

[31] Klemenic, *op. cit.*

[32] Most newer contracts have market price features, and thus actual prices for future delivery are highly uncertain. Also, while market prices must, in equilibrium, reflect marginal production costs, the only presently available market price for uranium is a spot price which can be both extremely volatile and a function of very short-term supply and demand relationships.

escalation (above the average inflation rate) in the near term, uranium pricing is undoubtedly affected to some extent by price trends of other energy commodities. A rise in oil prices to the $20-per-barrel level, for instance, now widely predicted to occur by 1980, would certainly have some effect on uranium price trends.

The Question of Uranium Imports

While it is difficult to draw definitive conclusions in the light of conflicting and rapidly changing estimates of both the supply of, and the demand for, resources, the considerations outlined to this point suggest the strong possibility that the United States will require substantial imports of uranium to supplement domestic supplies at some point in the 1980s.

It is clearly in the interest of the United States to cultivate those potential foreign suppliers that are most secure in terms of producibility, of actual and potential resources, and of political and economic stability. On the basis of these considerations, Canada offers an optimal source of supply. It should be remembered that in the 1957-67 period when the USAEC was procuring large amounts of uranium, the Canadian component of U.S. imports — which, in some years, made up half of U.S. requirements — was a very large one. In 1959, for instance, of over 33,000 tons purchased by USAEC, 45.2 percent was of U.S. origin, 40.7 percent of Canadian origin, and 14.1 percent from other countries. If Canada were to capture 50 percent of the U.S. market for imported uranium, it would mean a potential level of exports of Canadian uranium to the United States in the area of several thousand tons of oxide per year during the 1980s. The absence of barriers to trade in nuclear fuel materials on both sides would be a necessary condition for such trade.

The likelihood that this level of exports could be available from Canada over the period from the early 1980s to the end of the century, in the light of Canadian resources, productive capacity, and domestic and foreign commitments, will be examined in the next chapter.

4

Canada As a Uranium Supplier

While it is likely that sufficient uranium resources will be found in the United States to provide for the bulk of its domestic nuclear power needs for this century, there are strong possibilities that, some time after 1980, substantial quantities of imported uranium will be required. The examination of the Canadian reserves picture in this chapter suggests that a significant part of that requirement could be supplied by Canada.

Canadian Reserves Estimates

The Uranium Resource Appraisal Group of Energy, Mines and Resources Canada prepares annual studies of the Canadian uranium supply and demand situation, including reserve estimates. The June, 1976, report outlines a classification scheme for uranium resources that differs from both U.S. and international practice.[1] One of the most important distinctions is that Canada has retained classification by price range, based on rates of recovery consistent with currently proven mining and processing technology.

In the Canadian scheme, there are four official classes of uranium resources — measured, indicated, inferred, and prognosticated.

- Measured resources are proven reserves drilled and sampled to the point where the size, shape, and mineral content of the deposit are well established, and probable recovery factors demonstrated.
- Indicated resources have been similarly investigated, but there are sufficient uncertainties in the data to prevent a complete delineation or assay of the deposit.
- Inferred or possible resources comprise estimates based on the geology of the deposit rather than on sampling; the deposit must lie within 2,000 feet of measured or indicated resource deposits.
- Prognosticated resources are geologically inferred resources outside the 2,000-foot limit.

---

[1] Energy, Mines and Resources Canada, *1975 Assessment of Canada's Uranium Supply and Demand* (Ottawa: Supply and Services Canada, 1976).

Measured and indicated resources are equivalent to the international NEA-IAEA classification of "reasonably assured resources" mentioned in Chapter 3. They equate to "reserves" in U.S. terminology. Inferred and prognosticated resources equate to the international "estimated additional resources." The definition of "speculative" resources — outside known uranium-bearing areas — is similar to the U.S. definition. However, speculative resources are not included as part of Canada's resource estimates.

If Canadian "price" categories are equated to ERDA "cost" categories on a "plus 33 percent" basis, then Canadian resources available at below $20 a pound of U_3O_8 equate to resources at less than $15 in the ERDA classification, and resources available at a price of less than $40 equate to U.S. resources at a price of less than $30.

TABLE 2

Estimate of Canada's Recoverable Uranium Resources
(short tons U_3O_8)

	Mineable at		
Resources	Up to $20 per Pound U_3O_8	$20-40 per Pound U_3O_8	Total
Measured	82,000	14,000	96,000
Indicated	107,000	22,000	129,000
Inferred	226,000	111,000	337,000
Prognosticated	168,000	282,000	450,000
Total	583,000	429,000	1,012,000

Source: Energy, Mines and Resources Canada, *1975 Assessment of Canada's Uranium Supply and Demand* (Ottawa: Supply and Services Canada, 1976), p. 3.

As Table 2 shows, Canadian low-cost reserves at the end of 1975 were 189,000 short tons of U_3O_8, and high-cost reserves were 36,000 tons, for a total of 225,000 tons. "Potential resources" (inferred plus prognosticated) totaled 787,000 tons. All told, Canada has just over one million tons of reasonably assured and estimated uranium resources, only one-third those of the United States, as tabulated in the NURE report.

With a smaller energy economy and a more uranium-economical power-reactor system, however, Canada uses only a small proportion of its own uranium — just 500 tons in 1975, or less than 10 percent of shipments of 6,126 tons in that year. And since Canada has a much less intensively explored territory that is considerably greater in extent than the continental United States, the prospects of discovering new uranium reserves at present price levels are much better.

Uranium-Bearing Areas of Canada

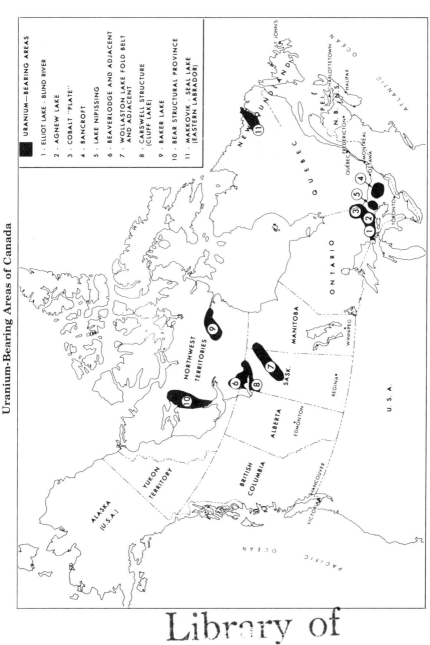

URANIUM—BEARING AREAS

1 · ELLIOT LAKE · BLIND RIVER

2 · AGNEW LAKE

3 · COBALT "PLATE"

4 · BANCROFT

5 · LAKE NIPISSING

6 · BEAVERLODGE AND ADJACENT

7 · WOLLASTON LAKE FOLD BELT
    AND ADJACENT

8 · CARSWELL STRUCTURE
    (CLUFF LAKE)

9 · BAKER LAKE

10 · BEAR STRUCTURAL PROVINCE

11 · MAKKOVIK · SEAL LAKE
     (EASTERN LABRADOR)

Source: Energy, Mines and Resources Canada, *1975 Assessment of Canada's Uranium Supply and Demand* (Ottawa: Supply and Services Canada, 1976), p. 2.

The Location of Reserves

The geology of Canadian uranium deposits is quite different from that in the United States; and partly as a result, so is the structure of the uranium-mining industry. The locations of the eleven uranium-producing areas discovered to date in Canada are shown on the accompanying map (Figure 3), and a list of producing mines and their capacity is given in Table 3.

TABLE 3

Uranium-Milling Plants in Canada, January, 1977

	Location	Nominal Capacity (short tons of ore per day)
Active		
Denison Mines Limited		
Denison Mill	Elliot Lake, Ontario	7,100
Eldorado Nuclear Limited	Eldorado, Saskatchewan	1,800
Rio Algom Mines Limited		
Quirke Mill	Elliot Lake, Ontario	7,100
Gulf Minerals Canada Limited	Rabbit Lake, Saskatchewan	2,000
Madawaska Mines Limited	Bancroft, Ontario	1,500
Kerr Addison Mines Limited	Agnew Lake, Ontario	1,300[a]
Inactive[b]		
Preston Mines Limited	Elliot Lake, Ontario	3,000
Rio Algom Mines Limited		
Nordic Mill	Elliot Lake, Ontario	3,700
Panel Mill	Elliot Lake, Ontario	3,000
Denison Mines Limited		
Stanrock Mill	Elliot Lake, Ontario	3,000

[a] Bacterial leaching, no mill required.

[b] Capacities listed refer to capacities at time of closure; other previously operating mills have been dismantled.

Source: R. M. Williams, *Uranium Supply to 2000: Canada and the World* (Ottawa: Energy, Mines and Resources Canada, 1976), p. 22.

The most extensive and productive deposit is in quartz-pebble conglomerate beds in the Elliot Lake region near the north shore of Lake Huron. Denison Mines Limited and Rio Algom Mines Limited have been mining the deposits since the 1950s and expect to continue until well past the year 2000.

The Bancroft area was one of the first where uranium was discovered. The uranium occurs in pegmatite bodies in granite and is generally of lower grade than the Elliot Lake deposit. There are several mines that have been dormant since their USAEC contracts expired, but one of them, the Canadian Faraday Mine, has been reopened by Madawaska Mines Limited and is currently re-entering production.

A similar pegmatite deposit at Kitts-Michelin on the Labrador peninsula is being investigated by a joint venture of Brinex, a British-Newfoundland Corporation subsidiary, and Urangesellschaft, a German exploration company. It is in the early stages of development.

Eldorado Nuclear Limited, a Canadian crown corporation, recovers uranium from pitchblende-bearing veins near the north shore of Lake Athabasca. This area has the distinction of being the first in North America to be mined for radioactive elements. Radium was mined from pitchblende deposits on the eastern shore of Great Bear Lake in the 1930s.

A row of new discoveries in the past few years has been developed in northern Saskatchewan, south of Lake Athabasca — Key Lake, Cluff Lake, and Rabbit Lake. Two of the three deposits lie on the edge of the Athabasca sandstone region, which also extends into northern Alberta. Key Lake, being developed by a consortium of German and U.S. interests and the provincial government (Uranerz, Inexco, and the Saskatchewan Mining Development Corporation), has a very small mineralized zone but is remarkably rich, with ore grading up to 13.3 percent uranium. Cluff Lake is also a rich deposit, grading up to 10 percent. Development of Cluff Lake by Amok Ltée., a French exploration company, is awaiting the report of a provincial commission at time of writing. This will be discussed later. Last year Gulf Minerals Canada, in conjunction with Uranerz, began operating a mine at Rabbit Lake with an annual production of 1,900 tons.

All this new development does not exhaust promising areas of Canada. PNC Limited, representing Japanese interests, is drilling in the Beaverdell area of British Columbia; and a Denison-sponsored company is drilling near Birch Island, British Columbia. At Baker Lake, in the Northwest Territories, Cominco, Uranerz, Shell, and Urangesellschaft are active. One hole drilled in the area averaged 2.3 pounds of uranium per ton over a 372-foot depth. Imperial Oil is exploring north of Great Bear Lake and even as far as the Cape Dorset area of Baffin Island.

Unlike oil and gas, uranium is a promising mineral for exploration in remote areas. As long as it is possible to get heavy equipment in, and provided there is sufficient production for a mill, the concentrate is so valuable that there is no economic problem in getting it to market.

The difference between the U.S. and the Canadian industries is suggested by the fact that the mills of five operating Canadian producers have a nominal capacity of 19,400 tons of ore daily, while the seventeen operating U.S. mills owned by fifteen companies have a nominal capacity only slightly greater. U.S. uranium operations, many of which are open-pit, are typically quite small, with ore trucked to a nearby mill (sixteen mills in the western United States service the two hundred major producers). The typical Canadian operation is a large underground mine, with its own mill and concentrator facilities and, usually, a whole town (such as Uranium City, Saskatchewan) built around it.

Based on present developments, annual Canadian uranium productive capacity will rise from 7,600 tons U₃O₈ to 15,000 tons by 1984. At that time the industry will have regained the productive capacity it had in 1959, when 14,850 tons was shipped from Beaverlodge, Quirke, and Denison Mines.

The Role of Government

The Canadian uranium industry has been conducted from the beginning in delicate balance among the Canadian government, which owns Eldorado Nuclear; a major international mining corporation, Rio Algom Mines Limited (a member of the Rio Tinto group); and Denison Mines Limited, a native Canadian company. When Denison Mines appeared to be on the point of selling out to foreign interests in 1970, during the first sign of a recovery of interest in uranium, the federal government stepped in with legislation to prevent the sale, and foreign ownership is now limited to 33 percent of any uranium producer. As a result, new uranium developers in Canada tend to be partnerships. Such consortiums typically consist of a foreign consumer (public or private), an expert mine developer (either foreign or native), and a government body. French and German participation has already been mentioned. The Italian government is exploring in Canada via AGIP Explorations Limited, and the Japanese government via Power Reactor and Nuclear Fuel Development Corporation (the parent of PNC Limited). The Spanish utility consortium, ENUSA, and the British Central Electricity Generating Board are also involved. Canadian branches of multinational energy companies — Gulf Oil, Imperial Oil, and Canadian Occidental Petroleum — are all active in exploration. Smaller Canadian mining and energy companies are also involved. Corporate uranium exploration spending in Canada reached $50 million in 1976, about 38 percent of all mineral exploration excluding hydrocarbons.[2]

While federal government participation has been a fact of life for the uranium industry since its beginning, newer developments will have substantial participation by provincial governments. The

[2] Figures are from N. M. Ediger, "Canadian Uranium: The New Economics," address to the International Conference on Uranium, Geneva, September 14, 1976.

governments of Saskatchewan and Manitoba claim a right to up to 50 percent participation in any exploration venture in their provinces, on a shared-cost basis, through provincial mining development corporations. The two large public utilities in central Canada, Ontario Hydro and Hydro-Québec, and two Quebec crown corporations, Soquem and James Bay Development Corporation, are also participating in exploration.

As well as participating directly via Eldorado Nuclear, the Canadian federal government is spending $2.5 million per year on a ten-year reconnaissance program, begun in 1977 by the Geological Survey of Canada, to map 70 percent of the country on a five-kilometer grid for surface shows of radioactive minerals. Flatter areas will be examined by airborne gamma ray spectrometers, and geochemistry will be employed in more mountainous areas. While the program is not intended to make any uranium strikes itself, it should help the industry delineate the "haystacks" it would be profitable to explore for "needles." It has been estimated that just following up on the Geological Survey program will take $500 million worth of detailed geological investigation by private enterprise. This figure does not include development work on any attractive prospects found, which might require billions.

Foreign Investment Policy

To provide this kind of high-risk investment, Canada has traditionally looked to foreign sources of capital. The United States, because of the emphasis on building up its own uranium mining industry in the past decade, has not been dominant in Canadian uranium investment, which has come mainly from offshore. But overseas investment of exploration capital has been most readily available from government and utility interests, who were not inclined to back Canadian uranium plays unless they could gain access to at least a substantial part of the anticipated production. As N. M. Ediger has pointed out:

> These organizations are motivated by the desire to ensure long term supply as well as the prospect of an attractive rate of return on their risk capital. . . . It is reasonable to suppose that sustained aggressive exploration will result in significant discoveries over the next five to ten years and lead to an increase in production capacity considerably beyond that projected.[3]

The present Canadian situation poses several problems for a foreign agency seeking to ensure against a uranium deficit by investing in exploration. These relate to the following areas:

- The federal government's export policy, which places a priority on securing reserves for the useful (thirty-year) life of any Canadian power reactor that may be built between now and the year 2000.

---

[3] *Ibid.*

- Federal and provincial government policies that strongly regulate uranium production, its financing, exploration rights, labour and safety practices, and the transportation, processing, and marketing of its product.
- Special taxation policy and government participation schemes that have already been developed in one province (Saskatchewan) and may emerge in others, now that uranium seems to be becoming a highly profitable commodity. This may blunt the aggressiveness of some explorers.
- The already strong presence of offshore purchasers of Canadian uranium, who were buying long before U.S. users were permitted by their own country's embargo to enter the market. These interests are now important factors in uranium exploration and development, and over 100,000 tons of uranium are committed to foreign sales over the next fifteen years, of which only about 15 percent are for U.S. customers.

The point should be stressed that there are two types of non-Canadian exploration groups working in Canada. One group includes the Japanese, French, and Germans (either private or quasi-national organizations), who are looking for supplies for their home markets. However, U.S.-based multinational energy companies and their Canadian subsidiaries, who are prepared to sell either domestically or internationally, are now becoming more active.

Ensuring an Adequate Domestic Supply

Since 1974, Canada's uranium-export program has been geared to ensuring a thirty-year domestic fuel supply for existing and committed reactors and for those planned for ten years into the future. This is an objective that will shift with changes in projections of domestic requirements, which by the year 2000 could theoretically reach 650,000 tons of reserves. As of June, 1976, "set-aside" reserves totaled 81,000 tons; of this amount, domestic utilities must maintain a contracted fifteen-year forward supply for operating and committed reactors. This represents 33,000 tons of U_3O_8 for the country's 11,900 MW of existing and committed 1986 capacity.

In fact, Canadian uranium marketers are not too worried about the set-aside provision, since the required reserves are still well short of current available reserves. The formula used in calculating the provision takes account of resources in measured, indicated, and inferred categories with weighting factors of 1.0, 0.8, and 0.7, respectively, or a total of 435,000 tons — five times the set-aside limit. Further, since the regulation defines the basis for reserves as "resources mineable at up to twice the world market price at the time of assessment," any increase in world uranium prices would correspondingly increase these reserves. Nevertheless, the Canadian government cautiously restricts export contracts to ten years forward, with conditional approval, subject to partial recall, for a further five years.

It now appears unlikely that Canadian domestic uranium requirements by 2000 will be anything like 650,000 tons. Ontario Hydro, with 90 percent of planned 1986 Canadian nuclear generation, has already been forced to "slip" two 3,000 MW projects by one year each, and a 3,400 MW station by two years, because of capital constraints. While it does not appear that the Canadian nuclear program will suffer the erosion of U.S. nuclear construction, utilities in Canada have experienced reduced rates of load growth and are trimming their programs.

Special Export Problems

One current problem with the export of Canadian uranium is the concern of the Canadian government to serve the cause of non-proliferation of nuclear weapons technology. Adherence by the governments of all foreign customers to the U.N. Non-Proliferation Treaty (NPT), plus strict bilateral safeguards agreements, are mandatory conditions of export licensing. This resulted in the temporary suspension on January 1, 1977, of Canadian uranium shipments to all customers except Finland (which has signed the NPT), Spain (under old contracts), and the United States (with which Canada has a special "interim agreement"). It is not anticipated that this will be a major barrier to uranium exports in the long term, though it may present a barrier to exports to such countries as Argentina, which recently announced it would not adhere to the NPT. During these negotiations some participants felt that Canada was being disingenuous in its role, and there were reports that safeguards negotiations were being used to open up existing contracts to more generous price-escalation provisions. At one point it appeared that some major customers would be resistant enough to the Canadian position to turn elsewhere, which could lead to some redirection of export markets for Canadian uranium in the next year or two. An interim three-year agreement has now been signed between Canada and the European Economic Community, and permits for exports of Canadian uranium are now being granted. A similar agreement with Japan has also been signed.

The interim agreement under which Canada continues to export uranium to U.S. customers is that ERDA takes custody of the uranium on behalf of the U.S. government until such time as adherence to the NPT is formally ratified (probably within the year). The material in custody can then be transferred to the ultimate customer (usually a U.S. utility).

The Canadian government appears to be anticipating that uranium will be an important export commodity for Canada in the long term. This is indicated by the plans of government-owned Eldorado Nuclear Limited to build an export-dedicated $85 million refinery near Port Granby, Ontario, by 1980, with a capacity of 13,500 tons of uranium hexafluoride annually. Uranium hexafluoride (UF$_6$) is a compound of uranium used in diffusion plants as feed for enrichment. Being of no use to the Canadian nuclear program, its entire production will be exported. (Eldorado presently produces 4,500 tons of uranium fluoride at its Port Hope refinery.) This is consonant with Canadian government policy of maximum upgrading of resource products exported from Canada.

Provincial Regulations: A Disincentive?

Foreign customers for Canadian uranium in the next few years may find that provincial rather than national policies are impeding development of possible Canadian sources of uranium supply.

A case in point has recently been provided by the province of Saskatchewan, where there have been three important uranium discoveries since 1970. Each province has its own tax and royalty system with respect to natural resources, and Saskatchewan has developed heavy taxation regimes on its resource industries — first in the case of oil and gas, and then more recently in that of potash. In 1976 the legislature passed an amendment to the Mineral Resources Act which imposed a tax on mine profits, in addition to a royalty of 3 percent of gross sales. The tax on operating profits is 15 percent when the ratio of operating profit to capital investment is between 15 and 25 percent; 30 percent of profits in the range 25 to 45 percent; and 50 percent of all profits in excess of these rates. In addition, the royalty and the tax cannot be deducted as expenses in calculating federal corporation taxes. As N. M. Ediger points out: "The combined effect of federal corporate income tax, and the provincial royalty regime, is that up to 84 cents of every incremental dollar achieved through increased productivity or prices, will be stripped away by governments ... the share of cash flow allowed the entrepreneur ... becomes very small indeed. Small as that may be, I must say that governments have been very careful to avoid killing the golden goose — the goose is just a lot thinner."[4]

After announcing plans to develop the Cluff Lake, Saskatchewan, property and obtaining federal authorization to do so, Amok Ltée. suspended its plans in light of the province's announced intention to hold a series of environmental hearings on the effect of uranium-mining operations on the province and as to whether, in fact, the development of local uranium exploitation was in the social and economic interests of the province. The hearings commenced late in the spring of 1977 and continued into the fall. While at the time of writing the committee had not yet reported, its proceedings suggested that the Saskatchewan government is anxious to have a

---

[4] *Ibid.*

uranium industry in the province, if only for the purpose of generating more tax revenues from the resource sector. However, concern was shown during the hearings that some assurance be given by uranium developers that Saskatchewan's uranium will not contribute towards either further nuclear proliferation in the world at large or environmental deterioration in the province.

Especially if uranium prices continue to escalate, it is possible that other Canadian provinces and U.S. states will impose similar royalty and taxation schemes upon new uranium-extraction operations. New Mexico, for instance, has levied a 5 to 8 percent *ad valorem* tax on local uranium production, based on spot-market prices.

The Global Market

In spite of federal and provincial hurdles to uranium exports, Canada appears to be a most promising area for investment in new uranium developments in the next twenty-five years, in comparison to jurisdictions with comparable uranium deposits. Chart 4, which summarizes the world's known resources of uranium, indicates that Canada is surpassed only by the United States and Australia in the possession of low-cost (up to $15 per pound) resources.

Although Australia has no nuclear power program of its own, very large deposits of low-cost uranium have been discovered in the Northern Territory in the past few years. So far, Australia's only developed uranium property is the Mary Kathleen Mine, but development should be spurred on by the recent lifting of the four-year ban on uranium mining, during which a government commission studied the moral and environmental problems of uranium mining and use. Present plans call for annual production to reach 2,000 tons by 1981 and 10,000 tons by 1985, although industry sources think this may be too ambitious.[5] One major uncertainty about future supplies from Australia is that the Labour Party, which has held office about half the time since the thirties, has declared itself against any new uranium development until world safeguard problems have been resolved and has agreed not to interfere with existing exports only if no new mines were started. It has also been stated that a future Labour government would not feel bound to honour any new uranium contracts approved by the present Country Party government. Nevertheless, Australia can be expected to make a significant contribution to the world's uranium supply at some point in the 1980s.

Over the long term, the outlook for uninterrupted uranium exports from other major reserve holders is not promising. Sweden bulks large in high-cost reserves, but these reserves are all on surface beds of black shale, the exploitation of which would entail se-

---

[5] *Globe and Mail*, August 27, 1977.

CHART 4

Reasonably Assured World Uranium Resources, January 1, 1975
(thousand short tons U₃O₈)

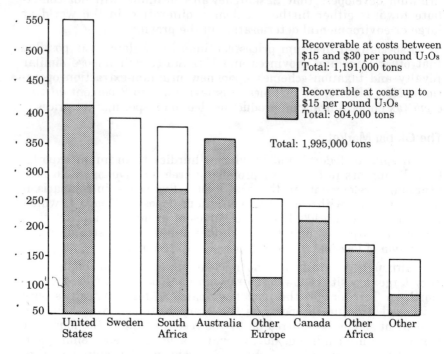

Source: Nuclear Energy Authority/International Atomic Energy Agency, *Uranium Resources, Production, and Demand* (Vienna, 1975).

vere environmental problems and very high costs. So far, no production is contemplated, and the reserves cannot be considered an addition to the world supply in the near future.

As indicated earlier, producibility may be an even more important factor than reserves in projecting supply. Figures on actual productive capacity now, and projected in 1985, appear even more favourable to the Canadian position than figures based on simple estimates of reserves (see Chart 5). While it would appear from the chart that South African production will overtake Canadian production by 1985, a large part of South Africa's supply is generated as a by-product of the notoriously unstable gold-mining industry. The rest, the Rossing deposit, is located in Namibia, an area whose future promises to become increasingly unstable politically. The same can be said for Niger's ambitious plans; and most of its production is likely to be committed to France. Australia, even if the present deadlock on uranium exports is unblocked, would provide only 9,000

CHART 5

Annual World Uranium Production Capacities,[a] 1975-85
(thousand short tons U₃O₈ per year)

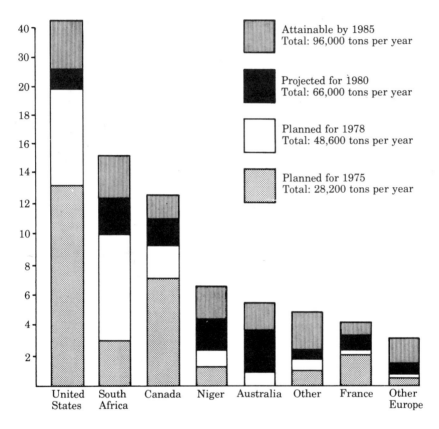

[a] Based on reserves as of January 1, 1975, and assuming availability of labour, equipment, finances, markets, and adequate lead time.

Source: Nuclear Energy Authority/International Atomic Energy Agency, *op. cit.*, p. 7.

exportable tons annually by 1985, some of which is already contracted for.

Canada, then, is the only country, with the exception of Australia, likely to have a large, dependable, stable, exportable surplus in 1985. Assuming that sufficient reserves are found to prevent the set-aside clause from locking up production, Canada could well have an exportable surplus (including existing export contracts) in a range upward of 10,000 tons of U₃O₈ annually by 1985. The substantial contracts Ontario Hydro signed in December, 1977, and

CHART 6

Annual Canadian Uranium Production, 1976-2000

(thousand short tons U_3O_8)

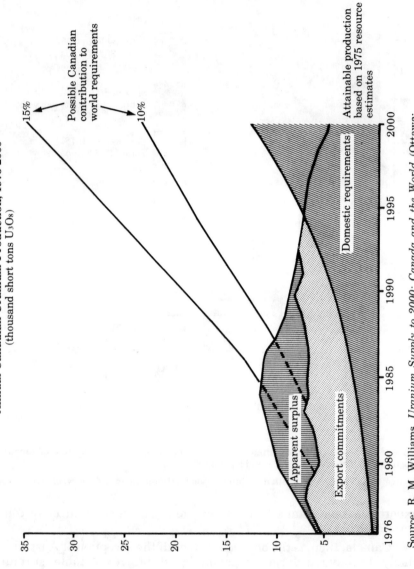

Possible Canadian contribution to world requirements

15%

10%

Apparent surplus

Export commitments

Domestic requirements

Attainable production based on 1975 resource estimates

Source: R. M. Williams, *Uranium Supply to 2000: Canada and the World* (Ottawa: Energy, Mines and Resources Canada, 1976), p. 16.

January, 1978, with Rio Algom Mines Limited, Denison Mines Limited, and Preston Mines Limited are intended for nuclear installations already in existence or planned and are part of the domestic requirements already projected in Chart 6.

At present, as was pointed out earlier, Canada has some 100,000 tons of forward uranium production tied up in contracts, some of which extend to 1992. Problems of the U.S. embargo on uranium imports have meant that only a comparatively small proportion of such forward contracts (about 15 percent) have been with U.S. customers. However, the general strategy of Canadian exporters interviewed for this study appears to be to place equal reliance on U.S., Japanese, and European (including U.K.) markets for Canadian uranium. Production from established areas is becoming increasingly committed to offshore contracts to the year 1990 and beyond.

Figures prepared by Energy, Mines and Resources Canada show that, without new discoveries, Canadian exportable surpluses tail off sharply about 1985. However, EMR documentation suggests that Canada could meet 10 percent of the rather inflated 1975 estimate of world requirements to the year 2000, given the discovery of five small, seven medium, and two large uranium strikes.[6]

In view of the cutback in U.S. nuclear expectations and the naturally overoptimistic projections of the underdeveloped countries, who can hardly afford to finance their own nuclear programs, the 1975 NEA-IAEA projections may well be overoptimistic by a factor of two.[7] This would enable Canada to supply 20 percent rather than 10 percent of the world market. Given a country the size of Canada and the success ratio of the rather limited uranium exploration programs of the past decade, such a target for the next twenty years does not seem at all unrealistic. One should note that this is a controversial and unprovable statement. It assumes, *inter alia*, that uranium prices will stay at a high level, that exploration will therefore be intensified, and that it will be successful.

It seems to coincide, however, with the present beliefs of uranium producers in Canada and with those of responsible officials of Energy, Mines and Resources Canada. Some Canadian utilities, however, express anxiety about ambitious export proposals that might decrease the availability of nuclear fuel for domestic programs. To this objection, it can be argued only that, should the rate of uranium discovery be unexpectedly disappointing, there should still be time to adjust long-term contracts in the light of supply expectations. Chart 6 shows that, given sufficient reserves to fulfill

---

[6] R. M. Williams, *Uranium Supply to 2000: Canada and the World* (Ottawa: Energy, Mines and Resources Canada, 1976), pp. 15-16.

[7] The recent WAES report estimates world annual uranium requirements as 230,000 tons maximum and 118,000 tons minimum by the year 2000 (Report of the Workshop on Alternative Energy Strategies, *Energy: Global Prospects 1985-2000*, Carroll L. Wilson, Director [New York: McGraw-Hill, 1977]).

Canada's domestic set-aside requirements, the main bulk of "apparent surplus" Canadian uranium production occurs during the 1980-90 time span. This "bulge" provides close to 5,000 tons annually between 1980 and 1987. However, in view of the uncertainties of the next decade, it is possible that U.S. uranium import requirements might be much greater after 1987, when most of this bulge disappears. It is therefore logical for U.S. enterprises committed to nuclear development to begin negotiations for firm contracts with Canadian suppliers; which is, in part, what is now happening. It would also seem logical, as part of these arrangements, to place as great a stake in Canadian uranium exploration as the current regulatory climate allows.

As the winter of 1976-77 showed, Canada can be generous in energy exports when faced with the clear and urgent need of its neighbour to the south. However, the uranium industry is far less flexible and operates upon a much longer-term marketing base than does the oil and gas industry. Rush supplies of uranium in the event of a critical nuclear fuel shortage in the United States would not be possible, owing to the difference in reactor systems.

The North American uranium situation provides a challenge for both Canada and the United States to work out a long-term strategy of mutually beneficial energy-materials exchange. Otherwise the pattern of the 1950s, of overurgent need stimulating overdevelopment, culminating in underutilization and the near collapse of an important Canadian resource industry, could recur in the 1980s.

5

Alternative Post-1985 Solutions

The difficulty of projecting the uranium supply picture more than a decade ahead is indicated by the many conflicting forecasts that exist and by the rapidity with which forecasts have changed in the past few years. In the face of these uncertainties we can examine in some detail the implications of various possible scenarios while remembering that we are constructing a set of extreme cases, no single one of which is likely to prevail completely at any one time, let alone for the whole twenty-five years under study. This chapter considers two basic scenarios and a number of variations on one of them.

First, there is the possibility that, by 1985, uranium prospecting will be highly successful and that technological and economic solutions will be found for the various problems inhibiting mine development, so that there will be a rapid increase in uranium production. This scenario assumes that the world uranium supply will be adequate for even optimistic levels of projected demand and that the price of uranium will not escalate, and may even decline in real terms.

Second, there is the prospect that exploration efforts on a world scale will not be massive enough and will be only modestly successful, resulting in a prolonged world shortage of uranium and continuing high prices, probably escalating to $75 a pound by 1985 and perhaps to well over $100 by the year 2000, in current dollars. Protracted uranium shortages and escalating prices could lead to at least three possible future developments:

• An intensive, well-directed program could have been initiated in the United States within the next couple of years to close the fuel cycle and develop some type of breeder alternative. However, given President Carter's energy policy, this does not appear likely.

• The United States will be forced in the next few years into a thorough reappraisal of its whole energy program. It might scrap its present reliance on nuclear power as a primary energy source, relying instead on massive deployment of the still-impressive coal reserves of the nation to provide electrical power. There are many anti-nuclearists who would consider this a favourable outcome.

• Energy authorities could turn their backs on twenty years of nuclear development and abandon light-water reactors in favour of the thermal converter, probably of the CANDU or organic-cooled, natural-uranium type. This would achieve a long-term saving of 40 percent of the uranium requirements of new stations and would ease the load on enrichment facilities. A variant of, or a supplement to, such a program would be to undertake a joint program to site a number of large CANDU-type stations along the Canadian side of the border whose output would, by agreement, be dedicated to supplying a portion of baseload requirements for the northern United States.

In view of all that has been said concerning the current disarray and confusion in world uranium markets, the first scenario seems most unlikely. Even with a maximum credible buildup of domestic production capacity, it would appear that the United States will move away from a position of self-sufficiency in uranium supply some time early in the 1980s. Consequently, the remainder of this chapter will examine the various possibilities implied by the second scenario.

Fuel Recycling: An Option Foreclosed

While President Carter's policy decisions to suspend previous U.S. programs to reprocess spent fuel and to develop fast-breeder reactors may be reversed by his, or a subsequent, Administration, it is clear that both programs will be delayed indefinitely.

Carter's energy program is a reversal of his earlier preference for internationalization of fuel-recycling development. In May, 1976, he told the United Nations:

> It makes no economic sense to locate national reprocessing facilities in a number of different countries... [since] the co-location of reprocessing, fuel fabrication, and fuels storage facilities would reduce the risks of weapons proliferation, theft of plutonium during transport, and environmental contamination.[1]

Because the United States has more expertise than do other nations in reprocessing, the President said that it should initiate a multinational program "designed to develop experimentally the technology, economics, regulations, and safe-guards to be associated with plutonium recovery and recycling. The program should be developed by the U.S. in cooperation with the International Atomic Energy Agency."[2] President Carter also suggested that the Allied-General Barnwell plant "could become the first multinational reprocessing facility under the auspices of IAEA. Separated plutonium might ultimately

---

[1] *Daily Oil Bulletin*, April 25, 1977, p. 3.
[2] "The President's Stand on Energy," *Mainliner*, December, 1976.

be made available to all nations on a reliable, cheap, and nondiscriminatory basis after blending with natural uranium."[3]

But while the United States may originally have had the lead in reprocessing and plutonium-separation technology during the days of secret weapons programs, the Europeans have not been idle. Great Britain, of course, has operated a nuclear-fuel-reprocessing plant at Windscale for three decades for both metallic and oxide fuels. The oxide section of the plant was shut down in 1973 after an "incident" and has not been operating recently. The French atomic energy agency, CEA, is operating a large reprocessing plant for uranium oxide at La Hague. Another plant, at Mol, Belgium, has been turned over to Eurochemie, a branch of the European Nuclear Energy Agency, and the Italians have a pilot reprocessing plant at Saluggia. None of these plants are as large as the 1,500-tons-a-year Barnwell operation — they total about 600 tons a year in capacity — but as both knowledge of, and investment in, reprocessing techniques become increasingly diffused, any likelihood of "co-location" of facilities under the IAEA becomes increasingly doubtful.

At some point in the future, as the once-through fuel cycle eats up more and more uranium, there will be increasing pressure to reprocess the U.S. inventory of spent fuel. The longer that closing of the fuel cycle is put off, the greater will be the effort required to resume it. As well as the "pull" of demand for fissile material, there is the "push" of scarcity for spent-fuel storage. As this expensively stored inventory of fissile material builds up, pressure will mount to recycle it, with the smaller volumes of active liquid waste from reprocessing being solidified in a chemically inert form and disposed of by means of non-retrievable storage in deep geological formations. Public authority can move rapidly when the need is demonstrated graphically enough. The governor of Ohio, for instance, abruptly reopened permits for offshore drilling on the eastern half of Lake Erie in February, 1977, after a six-year moratorium for environmental reasons. All it took to convince him of the urgency was the 1976-77 winter's state-wide gas shortage that closed businesses and laid off hundreds of thousands of working voters. (Ironically, it will be several years before any gas found becomes available.)

Nuclear developments, however, cannot be turned on and off that quickly. Even with the heavily funded programs envisioned in 1975, ERDA did not foresee operation of the Barnwell facility or completion of the breeder-reactor prototype at Clinch River until the 1980s. Another decade would have been required until the buildup of such facilities could have made an appreciable impact on nuclear fuel requirements. The inevitable loss of momentum from the suspension of both projects makes it most likely that, even if reacti-

---

[3] "Latest Nuclear Planning Points to Major Changes," *Chemical Week*, November 17, 1976, p. 18.

vated, they could not be ready until the late 1980s and therefore would have negligible effects on uranium-demand curves before the end of the century.

Is Coal the Solution?

One option for the United States, faced with an insufficient supply of nuclear fuel, is to tail off nuclear development altogether and place reliance upon its still-impressive coal reserves.

There are many vocal opponents of the nuclear power program who would advocate this course and propose that the United States turn to its massive reserves of coal as the major source of primary fuel for electricity generation. To replace the anticipated 510,000 MW nuclear capacity as well as anticipated coal-fired capacity of the United States by the year 2000 would require burning 40 billion tons of coal on a cumulative basis over the period 1977-2000, in 500 thermal stations of conventional size.[4] This is 20 percent of the total economic resources of coal in the United States, according to the National Petroleum Council. The mining of this coal would require strip mining of many thousands of square miles and would impose a burden of two billion tons of sulphur dioxide on the atmosphere or, alternatively, an investment of $130 billion in 1975 dollars in precipitation equipment.[5] The burning of this much coal would contribute, ironically, many hundreds of times more radiation to the atmospheric background than equivalent power production from nuclear plants because coal and lignite are natural absorbents for trace uranium compounds in ground water, and these are released when coal is burned. None of these considerations rule out coal as a solution: they merely suggest that alternatives be examined on the basis of economics.

The relative cost differentials between coal and nuclear power vary, and will continue to vary, among different regions. Mine-mouth generation of power from thermal coal will be competitive for many years in the northwestern United States, which, at present, however, is not a power-short area. As already pointed out, the balance between the two fuels will shift, not because of the price of uranium, but mainly because of changes in the price of capital goods and of coal.

From an economic viewpoint, there is no question that nuclear power is demonstrably the lowest-cost solution to the energy needs of many areas of the United States. But the advantage varies from

---

[4] This estimate was provided by M. A. Kane, fuel-planning engineer with Ontario Hydro, in private communication with the author.

[5] A recent study by Drexel Burnham Lambert of New York points out that less than one-third of U.S. coal reserves meet federal sulphur-content standards for new coal-fired plants, and of this one-third, 87 percent is in the West, remote from industrial centres (reported in *Coal Week*, April 25, 1977).

area to area. A study in January, 1977, by National Economic Research Associates projected that the average total cost of generation for a power plant at Blythe, California, would be 46.4 mills (1985 dollars) per kilowatt-hour, while the average generating cost of a coal-fired plant would be 62.3 mills.[6] A similar study of two North Carolina utilities, however, suggests that the analysis is sensitive to the size of the system. For Duke Power, the larger of the two systems, the estimated 1975 generating cost was 17.7 mills per kilowatt-hour for nuclear, and 22.8 for coal. For Carolina Light and Power, the difference was much less: 22.9 mills for nuclear and 23.9 for coal.[7]

The Prospects for Conversion to More Efficient Reactor Technologies

Given a long, continued shortage of uranium, the other alternative would be for the United States to step away from its thirty-year tradition of uranium-fueled light-water reactors and to take fundamentally new directions in the technology of power reactors. One option, as suggested by the U.S. Administration's recent energy policy statement, would be to move to advanced converter reactors. The two major types of converters available are the Canadian heavy-water moderated reactor and the high-temperature, gas-cooled reactor. Such a shift would not be an easy step to take, although both General Electric and Westinghouse, the major U.S. nuclear suppliers, have acquired know-how in heavy-water-reactor technology through their Canadian subsidiaries.

A second option would be to develop new fuel combinations that would extend the energy that could be derived from a given amount of fissionable material. Two possibilities are the "spiking" of natural uranium fuel with a small amount of plutonium and the development of a system using plutonium-thorium fuel.

If the United States chose to adopt the Canadian system, there would be no possibility it could buy CANDU reactors "off the shelf" from Canada. With six 750-megawatt units and four 500-megawatt units being developed for Ontario Hydro by 1985, and 600-megawatt units being developed in Quebec and New Brunswick, Canada's nuclear industry has all it can do to keep on schedule with existing projects. However, engineering for the CANDU power reactor is, if anything, somewhat less complex than for BWRs and PWRs, and Canadian designs could be produced fairly rapidly by established U.S. nuclear suppliers. Fuel could probably be fabricated in both countries. The limitations of Canadian industry are suggested by the fact that, of CANDU reactor systems produced so far, only about 75 percent by value of the components are made in Canada; alloy tubing,

---

[6] *Nucleonics Week*, January 27, 1977, p. 6.
[7] *Loc. cit.*

stainless steel plate of certain dimensions, fueling-machine components, and certain types of instrumentation are still imported. Yet
the $700-million-a-year existing market for CANDU equipment
corresponds to 20 percent of total annual Canadian production of all
industrial machinery in 1975.

The most probable scenario would be a partnership between
Canadian companies established in this field and U.S. companies. (In
many cases, as with Canadian General Electric and Canadian
Westinghouse, the Canadian company has a U.S. affiliate.) Presum-
ably, where the technology has been developed by Atomic Energy of
Canada Limited, licensing arrangements could be worked out.

In view of the length of time it would take for such an advanced
converter system to achieve any substantial reduction in overall
U.S. demand for uranium, it would seem to be of greater mutual
benefit to both countries to collaborate on the development of some
more advanced version of the heavy-water moderated reactor —
perhaps the organic-cooled heavy-water moderated reactor (OCR).
This type of reactor, as well as being more efficient than the
CANDU, opens the possibility of introducing the thorium near-
breeder cycle in the 1990s. The introduction of the thorium cycle
does not depend on the OCR, however; thorium can be introduced in
any heavy-water moderated reactor.

One specific limited U.S. application of the existing CANDU design is suggested by the possibility that spent fuel from a light-
water reactor might have a high enough residual activity to be
reused as fuel for a heavy-water moderated reactor. This would not
require any chemical reprocessing, but simply stripping the uranium
oxide from the sheathing of the spent-fuel element and "re-canning"
it in fuel bundles adapted to the CANDU. Several light-water reactors, it is calculated, could supply sufficient spent fuel to keep a
CANDU- of equivalent size running, without additional uranium.
There are differences of opinion on the feasibility of this suggestion,
but it would seem to deserve some further research and possible
piloting, since it not only economizes on uranium, but also alleviates
the spent-fuel-storage problem. (Pound for pound, CANDU spent fuel
has a much lower radioactivity than that from light-water reactors.)

The Canadian nuclear program, unlike that in the United
States, continues to push on towards the objective of closing the fuel
cycle and maintaining the option of adopting a near-breeder reactor
in the 1990s. A pilot plutonium-separation plant has been operating
at Chalk River Nuclear Laboratories of Atomic Energy of Canada
for some years, and natural uranium-fuel elements spiked with a
very small amount of plutonium (about one gram per kilo of
uranium) have already been used in Canadian power reactors. First
indications are that this mixed-oxide fuel will double the power
output or "burnup" over the life of a given amount of fuel from 6,800

megawatt-days per ton to about 13,600. U.S. reactors using enriched fuel achieve 20,000 to 30,000 megawatt-days per ton.

Canada could meet its domestic mixed-oxide-fuel requirements for a very modest investment in a chemical separation plant. Such a plant, producing only one ton of plutonium in 1985, could save 1,000 of the predicted 2,000 tons of uranium required to fuel domestic nuclear power stations in that year.[8] If the 1985 price of U₃O₈ is in the $65 range (in 1976 dollars) — which, extrapolating from 1980 quotations for forward delivery of $53.65, is quite credible — such an alternative would save nearly $300 million of uranium in that year.

Further, there is an even more potentially valuable application for plutonium. Mixed with thorium in a nuclear fuel, the neutrons from plutonium fission convert the thorium into another fissionable form of uranium, U-233. If U-233 were recovered from such spent-plutonium/thorium fuel and recycled, by the time equilibrium was reached, an entire CANDU system of 12,000 MW could be operated on a half dozen tons of thorium per year, with no further uranium requirements. Such a system would take some decades to reach equilibrium, however.

Dr. W. B. Lewis, previously Senior Vice President, Research, of Atomic Energy of Canada Limited and now on the faculty of Queen's University in Kingston, Ontario, has consistently backed a thorium-fueled variant of the CANDU, known as "CANDU-OC-Thorium." This is a thorium-uranium-plutonium near-breeder reactor using as a coolant an organic liquid of the terphenyl species (a kind of heavy "cooking oil") which remains liquid at over 400 degrees Celsius. The coolant is circulated to heat exchangers to produce steam at much higher temperatures than possible in the CANDU. Capital costs are lowered because expensive heavy water is used only as a moderator, and not as a coolant. In addition, because of the higher temperature of operation, station efficiency is increased to 39 percent from the present 29.1 percent efficiency of the Pickering-type CANDU reactor.[9]

Thorium is four times as common as uranium in the earth's crust and is frequently found in the same deposits. AECL has been successfully running an organic-cooled research reactor at Whiteshell, Manitoba, since 1966. By combining fuel reprocessing and the thorium cycle by the 1990s, Canada could cut its domestic uranium requirements to virtually zero. This would have a major

---

[8] S. R. Hatcher, "CANDU Fuel Cycle Alternatives: What Are They and Why Are We Interested?," paper presented to the Canadian Nuclear Association, Seminar on Canada Fuel Cycle Alternatives, Toronto, May 5, 1976.

[9] See W. B. Lewis, "Abundant Harnessed Energy at Low Cost and Low Risk from Nuclear Fission," Elizabeth Laird Memorial Lecture, University of Western Ontario, April 3, 1974.

impact on Canada's capacity to export uranium. Canada might also be able to benefit from the export of thorium-organic coolant technology.

"Exporting" the CANDU

A variant on U.S. adoption of the thermal reactor, which has been discussed during the past couple of years, is the possibility of using the CANDU on its native soil to provide contracted base-load electric power for population centres in the northern United States. Major industrial centres such as Boston, New York, Detroit, and Chicago are well within economic transmission range of the Canadian border. While this would not solve the basic U.S. energy problem, a substantial, if temporary, contribution to the U.S. electrical supply could be made in this way. About one-quarter of the U.S. demand for electricity is concentrated in the area of the eastern United States roughly 500 miles south of the border, which could conveniently be reached by existing transmission technology. Professor Aaron L. Segal of Cornell University suggested the idea at Project Independence hearings in New York City in 1975. The proposal is certainly a feasible one. In fact, the oil-fired Lorneville station near Saint John, New Brunswick, already provides about half its generation to the New England power grid under a five-year contract. Nevertheless, it might be difficult to set up a single organization for such a scheme. Each provincial utility in Canada is autonomous and is unlikely to want to raise capital for a power station for which most of the power will have to be dedicated to another user. Of course, both U.S. and Canadian utilities swap power during peak-load periods and have been doing so for years. There is no difficulty with the scheme from the viewpoint of the Federal Power Commission in the United States.

Ontario Hydro, the dominant generator of nuclear power among Canadian utilities, appears most interested in the possibility. From the viewpoint of this utility, it would be convenient to build CANDU stations early. Siting near the border would be no problem, since that is where the existing Ontario load centres are. Then it could sell contract power to U.S. northern-tier utilities in blocks, decreasing the volume over time as its own domestic load moved up. The incentive would be that U.S. utilities would provide the bulk of the capital financing for the station. A shortage of capital has forced Ontario Hydro to put back plans for two more nuclear stations by one year.

With modern techniques of load transfer, such an injection of Canadian power could make a contribution to demand a long way south of the border, with each utility passing from hand to hand, so to speak, the extra power from its own grid. To quote one Canadian utility executive who asked to remain anonymous, "Such an ar-

ALTERNATIVE POST-1985 SOLUTIONS

rangement should be looked upon as the export of a highly manu-
factured Canadian product — because that is what electricity is
today."

However, from the U.S. point of view, it is not likely that northern utilities would wish to depend on imports for a substantial frac-
tion of the system base load for any extended period. Also, CANDU
reactors cannot adjust easily to meet peaks and valleys in proven
demand. Because of the low reactivity of the fuel, they operate most
effectively if kept at the same power level most of the time and if
the power output is changed only slowly. This would mean that the
U.S. utilities would still have to provide the bulk of "peaking"
capacity.

One can imagine such an enterprise only on a temporary, declining basis to solve an imminent power shortage caused by a dearth
of either nuclear or conventional fuels in the United States. It
would, however, have the advantage of providing U.S. utilities with
a reliable source of power for a given term to permit them to adjust
generating capacities to a new situation.

Canadian Concerns over International Cooperation

This chapter indicates that, in addition to the likelihood of
Canada's being an important uranium supplier to the United States
in the future, there is also the strong possibility that the nuclear
programs of the two countries will be more closely related than in
the past. A discussion of possible opportunities for cooperation on
questions of fuel and technology forms the final chapter of this book.
By way of introduction, it should be noted that there are differences
of opinion in Canada about the extent to which it should be getting
involved in international nuclear cooperation.

Even though Canada's nuclear program appears to be pro-
ceeding smoothly relative to that in the United States, many Canadians feel that the nuclear industry in Canada should turn its eyes
inward. John Shephard, executive director of the Science Council of
Canada, recently advocated an industrial strategy that would transfer nuclear design and engineering from Atomic Energy of Canada
to a consortium embracing private companies and consultants as
well as provincial utilities.[10] He suggested that such a consortium
should ignore international markets, at least temporarily, and
concentrate on domestic efforts. If Canada does not further develop a
more hardnosed, private enterprise approach to nuclear business, he
feels, foreign competitors will take an increasingly large share of the
market for nuclear power equipment. This attitude has been stimulated by two recent events. First, there was the embarrassment of
having India, Canada's oldest nuclear pupil, with several CANDU

---

[10] *Energy Analects*, February 5, 1976, p. 5.

plants of its own, suddenly detonate a "peaceful nuclear device" in 1974. Second, there has been much public criticism of commissions paid by AECL to international agencies of dubious reputation to aid the offshore sale of nuclear reactors. There appears to be a growing feeling that the international exchange of nuclear technology, even that directed towards power generation, may not necessarily be profitable or even moral.

These concerns have not been shown to apply to Canada's relationship with the United States in any particular way, but they are still factors that could have implications for bilateral cooperation.

6

Opportunities for Cooperation

The energy crisis is clearly going to be a feature of life in both the United States and Canada for the foreseeable future. In both countries, dependence on petroleum resources must be reduced permanently in order to escape drastic economic dislocation. Caught between dwindling domestic resources of hydrocarbons and growing energy needs, neither country has much choice but to substantially increase the employment of nuclear energy in this century.

By postponing its efforts to close the fuel cycle and develop the fast breeder, it appears most likely that the United States will require imports of uranium in the range of several thousand tons per year beginning sometime in the 1980s and continuing for the rest of the century. Canada, meanwhile, seems likely to have similar quantities surplus to its requirements. If substantial quantities of Canadian uranium are to be available for the United States, however, they must come from newly developed deposits, since established producers, especially in the Elliot Lake area, have contracted most of their exportable production to Europe and Japan on contracts running, in some cases, to 1991. Unless U.S. buyers move soon, they may find considerable difficulty in obtaining long-term contracted supplies of Canadian uranium.

The Canadian and U.S. entities involved should recognize immediately that partnership and planning are the way to achieve the greatest mutual benefits from trade in uranium. Two very important areas for joint participation are the financing of exploration and mine development and the planning of such development in tune with a reasonably accurate prediction of demand. About 40 percent of the world's nuclear fuel demand until the year 2000 is expected to originate in the United States. Even though foreign equity participation in Canadian uranium-mining ventures has been limited to 33 percent, even minority partnerships, whether by U.S. resource companies seeking profitable investments or by utilities seeking to develop sources of supply, will give some confidence of a predictable and profitable market for Canadian-produced uranium. The Canadian uranium industry does not want a repeat of the boom-and-bust development of the 1950s stimulated by USAEC contracts.

One suggestion for joint U.S.-Canadian cooperation has been the creation of a North American uranium stockpile. While such a stockpile, as explained in Chapter 1, could not prevent long-term escalation of uranium prices, it might help to level out short-term fluctuations and could also provide a price floor in periods of possible oversupply and thus permit greater assurance in the development of medium-quality deposits.

While the advantages to the United States of the availability of Canadian uranium are obviously great, the benefit to Canada of such exports is equally substantial.

There are two ways to evaluate the national benefits of an expanding resource industry. One approach is to examine what taxes and royalties, extracted from the production of that commodity, accrue to local and national governments. Since legislative restrictions in Canada ensure that at least 66 percent of the equity of any uranium producer will be held in Canada and since government participation in the business is already substantial, there can be little argument that the great bulk of any earnings from the industry will be kept in this country and contribute to its economic welfare.

The other approach is to look at the industry's contribution to gross national product and to the health of the economy as a whole. If Canadian uranium production in 1980 reaches the anticipated level of 13,000 tons and the price is $55 per pound, then the value of production will be $1.43 billion. By 1985, uranium production will be worth $2 billion if output is 15,000 tons at a reasonably projected price of $65 per pound. Value of production does not give a direct measure of the contribution of an industry to gross national product because the value of production includes the cost of inputs such as materials and fuel. For the mining industry as a whole, the proportion of the value of production that makes a contribution to GNP is about 65 percent. The net contribution of 1985 uranium production to GNP, therefore, will probably be about $1.3 billion. The impact of uranium exports on Canada's international trade balance would be a positive contribution of $1.36 billion in 1980 and nearly $1.9 billion in 1985. This is calculated by deducting domestic consumption of about 1,000 tons in 1980 and 2,000 tons in 1985 from production estimates and adding $100 million from production of uranium hexafluoride for enrichment feed. Earnings from uranium exports after 1980 can be expected to offset almost half the anticipated net negative balance of international payments due to imports of crude oil into eastern Canada.

Common Concerns in Regulation

Lead times for major new energy enterprises are long; it takes nearly a decade from the decision to commit resources to actual production of either a large nuclear station or a new uranium mine.

However, most current problems in the nuclear field in both countries have arisen from decisions too long deferred, or purposes too easily deflected. As a consequence, there is a high degree of uncertainty in both nuclear power commitment and uranium-resource estimation and production. Both Canada and the United States, in spite of present differences in their technology and in the organization of their nuclear power establishments, share common concerns in regulation, in closing the fuel cycle, and in improving nuclear-generation technology. In an enterprise as complex as nuclear power generation, the mutually beneficial exchange of materials and technology demands two things: first, that each partner have a sense of the trend of future developments for the other and, second, that both parties participate in advance planning.

The regulatory problems affecting this exchange, since they affect all planning, would have to be tackled first. On the national level, they do not appear massive. Adherence by the United States to the Non-Proliferation Treaty, the major requirement set by the Canadian government on exports of uranium, appears to be close to being resolved. In addition, the U.S. embargo on foreign uranium imports for domestic use is being phased out rapidly enough that it should not affect U.S. utilities' desire to obtain Canadian uranium supplies. Meanwhile, at state and provincial levels, the application of increasing levels of resource taxation upon uranium producers is taking place in both countries, and the uncertainty this imposes upon mining development is clearly a problem that will have to be worked out on a case-by-case basis.

A more urgent consideration is the use being made of the legislative process by public-interest groups to delay each new nuclear-plant-building and -operation permit to the greatest degree possible. This has up to now afflicted nuclear plants in the United States and is likely to impose a similar delay on an important uranium-mine project in Saskatchewan. Partly because of differences in Canadian legislation, but largely because of differences in technology, and perhaps because of the expertise in "soft sell" accumulated by Ontario Hydro, reactor programs have not so far been significantly delayed by public pressure in Canada. However, discussion of long-term storage and reprocessing policy during the next year or so promises to be stormy.

In view of the cost imposed on the U.S. nuclear and energy program in general by these extensive delays, it would seem appropriate to convene a federal-state conference on nuclear regulatory legislation. The main agenda would be to explore ways to allow the public the input and information that justified concern about safety and environmental questions requires, while preventing the kind of interminable intervention and appeals and counterappeals that prolong, without resolving, such questions. A similar review of Atomic Energy Control Board regulations and procedures in Canada is already in progress. Perhaps contact between the two national regulatory organizations could provide some helpful insights.

Possibilities for Technology Exchange

In the area of the enhancement of nuclear technology, there are clearly a number of possibilities for U.S.-Canadian cooperation. While the United States has withdrawn for the time being from spent-fuel reprocessing and mixed-oxide-fuel development, it would be unfortunate if, straining for a perhaps unobtainable international agreement in these areas, Canada and the United States neglected in the meantime to explore the potential for specific projects of bilateral cooperation.

A really large possible joint development program would be the organic-cooled, thorium-fueled near-breeder reactor. Should that project catch the imagination of U.S. nuclear planners, it could provide nearly all the benefits the troubled fast-breeder program promised at its inception twenty years ago. A well-funded and expertly led program, perhaps starting with the existing organic-cooled Whiteshell reactor in Manitoba, could possibly result in a proven commercial prototype by 1995.[1] Certainly, such a prospect at least deserves a conference between Canadian and U.S. nuclear scientists and engineers. Even if U.S. skepticism about organic coolant should be so widespread as to preclude its consideration, the thorium cycle should at least be worth discussion. As suggested in Chapter 1, availability and producibility of thorium resources would be a logical starting point.

Another important joint enterprise that appears well worth pursuing is the proposal to provide Canadian nuclear-generated electricity as a temporary component of the base load for northeastern power utilities in the United States. An analysis of this proposal would require joint discussions among the utilities involved (perhaps only Ontario Hydro on the Canadian side) and the state and national agencies affected. At this point it appears highly unlikely that either Canada or Ontario would wish to dedicate nuclear stations on Canadian soil to U.S. energy requirements indefinitely. Yet even a temporary arrangement might produce considerable benefit to both countries. A consortium of U.S. utilities might propose to a Canadian utility (or group of utilities) that some post-1985 nuclear-plant projects be pushed forward by, say, four to five years. The full output could then be contracted to the U.S. utilities for a specific period of time — say, five to six years — with possible extensions as the conditions warranted. The Canadian utility would have the benefit of

---

[1] Such a possibility has been suggested in W. B. Lewis, "Attainable Ratings of CANDU-OC-Thorium Set by the Properties of Organic Liquid Coolant," *Annals of Nuclear Energy* (1975) 2: 779-86.

financial assistance in the building and operating of a reactor it needed. U.S. utilities would have, for a limited time, a large block of the base-load power required in the energy-deficient northeastern part of the country, thus acquiring valuable breathing space in which to define and develop their capital-investment programs.

Conclusions

The issues surrounding future uranium supply and nuclear power are extremely complex. They involve uncertain technology; complicated political decisions concerning operational safety, waste disposal, and the proliferation of nuclear weapons; and the risk of placing too much reliance on reserve estimates and future demand patterns based on conflicting and scanty information. However, this study has attempted to reveal some of the opportunities as well as the uncertainties. In the short run, Canada and the United States will both benefit if Canada becomes a significant supplier of uranium to the United States in the 1980s. Further into the future, more fuel-efficient nuclear reactors will be the key to a plentiful supply of atomic energy. In speculating on this indefinite future, there are many areas for Canada-U.S. cooperation. To tackle the problems in a coordinated fashion and as soon as possible will be to the considerable benefit of both countries.

FOOTNOTES TO THE STATEMENT

Shirley Carr, Julien Major, Donald Montgomery, and Joe Morris: The author states that "caught between dwindling domestic resources of hydrocarbons and growing energy needs, neither country has much choice but to substantially increase the employment of nuclear energy in this century."

We do not believe that there is enough evidence to conclude that Canada has no choice but to increase its commitment to nuclear power. Various Canadian energy authorities are currently in the process of conducting major new analyses on demand and supply aspects of all forms of energy, and until the data are in, no definitive conclusions can be drawn.

Julien Major and Donald Montgomery: We fail to see the benefits to Canada of speeding up our nuclear capacity in order to give the United States a "valuable breathing space for them [U.S. utilities] to define and develop their capital investment programs." The author is saying Canada should close off its options so that the Americans can keep theirs open.

MEMBERS OF THE CANADIAN-AMERICAN COMMITTEE

Co-Chairmen

ROBERT M. MacINTOSH
Executive Vice-President,
The Bank of Nova Scotia,
Toronto, Ontario

PHILIP BRIGGS
Executive Vice President, Metropolitan Life
Insurance Company, New York, New York

Vice-Chairmen

STEPHEN C. EYRE
Comptroller, Citibank, N. A., New York,
New York

ADAM H. ZIMMERMAN
Executive Vice President, Noranda Mines
Limited, Toronto, Ontario

Members

JOHN N. ABELL
Vice President and Director, Wood Gundy
Limited, Toronto, Ontario

R. L. ADAMS
Executive Vice President, Continental Oil
Company, Stamford, Connecticut

J. D. ALLAN
President, The Steel Company of Canada,
Limited, Toronto, Ontario

J. A. ARMSTRONG
President and Chief Executive Officer, Imperial Oil Limited, Toronto, Ontario

CHARLES F. BAIRD
President, INCO Limited, New York, New
York

IAN A. BARCLAY
Chairman, British Columbia Forest Products Limited, Vancouver, British Columbia

THOMAS D. BARROW
Director and Senior Vice President, Exxon
Corporation, New York, New York

MICHEL BÉLANGER
President and Chief Executive Officer, Provincial Bank of Canada, Montreal, Quebec

ROY F. BENNETT
President and Chief Executive Officer, Ford
Motor Company of Canada, Limited, Oak-
ville, Ontario

ROD J. BILODEAU
Chairman of the Board and Chief Executive
Officer, Honeywell Limited, Scarborough,
Ontario

ROBERT BLAIR
President and Chief Executive Officer, Al-
berta Gas Trunk Line Company Limited,
Calgary, Alberta

ARDEN BURBIDGE
Park River, North Dakota

NICHOLAS J. CAMPBELL, JR.
New York, New York

SHIRLEY CARR
Executive Vice-President, Canadian Labour
Congress, Ottawa, Ontario

W. R. CLERIHUE
Executive Vice-President, Corporate Staff,
Celanese Corporation, New York, New York

HON. JOHN V. CLYNE
MacMillan Bloedel Limited, Vancouver,
British Columbia

THOMAS E. COVEL
Marion, Massachusetts

J. S. DEWAR
President, Union Carbide Canada Limited,
Toronto, Ontario

JOHN H. DICKEY
President, Nova Scotia Pulp Limited,
Halifax, Nova Scotia

JOHN S. DICKEY
President Emeritus and Bicentennial Pro-
fessor of Public Affairs, Dartmouth College,
Hanover, New Hampshire

THOMAS W. diZEREGA
Vice President, Northwest Pipeline Corporation, Salt Lake City, Utah

WILLIAM EBERLE
Robert Weaver Associates, Boston, Massachusetts

*MARTIN EMMETT
President — International Operations,
Standard Brands, Inc., New York, New
York

A. J. FISHER
President and Chairman of the Board,
Fiberglas Canada Limited, Toronto, Ontario

ROBERT M. FOWLER
Chairman, Executive Committee, C. D.
Howe Research Institute, Montreal, Quebec

JOHN F. GALLAGHER
Vice President — International Operations,
Sears, Roebuck and Company, Chicago, Il-
linois

W. D. H. GARDINER
Vice Chairman, The Royal Bank of Canada,
Toronto, Ontario

PAT GREATHOUSE
Vice President, International Union, UAW,
Detroit, Michigan

70 MEMBERS

JOHN H. HALE
Executive Vice President, Finance, Alcan
Aluminium Ltd., Montreal, Quebec

A. D. HAMILTON
President and Chief Executive Officer, Dom-
tar Limited, Montreal, Quebec

JOHN A. HANNAH
Executive Director, World Food Council —
United Nations, New York, New York

ROBERT H. HANSEN
Senior Vice President — International,
Avon Products, Inc., New York, New York

JAMES A. HENDERSON
Executive Vice President, American Express Co., New York, New York

ROBERT H. JONES
President, The Investors Group, Winnipeg,
Manitoba

EDGAR F. KAISER, JR.
President and Chief Executive Officer,
Kaiser Resources Ltd., Vancouver, British
Columbia

JOSEPH D. KEENAN
President of Union Label & Service Trades
Department, AFL-CIO, Washington, D.C.

DONALD P. KELLY
President and Chief Executive Officer, Esmark, Inc., Chicago, Illinois

DAVID KIRK
Executive Secretary, The Canadian Federation of Agriculture, Ottawa, Ontario

LANE KIRKLAND
Secretary-Treasurer, AFL-CIO, Washington,
D.C.

C. CALVERT KNUDSEN
President and Chief Executive Officer,
MacMillan Bloedel Limited, Vancouver,
British Columbia

MICHAEL M. KOERNER
President, Canada Overseas Investments
Limited, Toronto, Ontario

*WILLIAM J. KORSVIK
Vice President, International Banking De-
partment, The First National Bank of
Chicago, Chicago, Illinois

J. L. KUHN
President and General Manager, 3M
Canada Limited, London, Ontario

*RONALD W. LANG
Director, Research and Legislation, Canadian Labour Congress, Ottawa, Ontario

HERBERT H. LANK
Director, Du Pont of Canada Limited,
Montreal, Quebec

EDMOND A. LEMIEUX
Commissioner, Hydro-Québec, Montreal,
Quebec

RICHARD A. LENON
Chairman and President, International
Minerals and Chemical Corporation, Liber-
tyville, Illinois

FRANKLIN A. LINDSAY
Chairman, Itek Corporation, Lexington,
Massachusetts

L. K. LODGE
Chairman and President, IBM Canada Ltd.,
Don Mills, Ontario

A. H. MASSAD
Director, Mobil Oil, and President, Exploration and Producing Division, Mobil Oil Corporation, New York, New York

JULIEN MAJOR
Executive Vice-President, Canadian Labour
Congress, Ottawa, Ontario

PAUL M. MARSHALL
Calgary, Alberta

FRANCIS L. MASON
Senior Vice President, The Chase Manhat-
tan Bank, New York, New York

DENNIS McDERMOTT
UAW International Vice President and Director for Canada, International Union, United Automobile, Aerospace and Agricul-
tural Implement Workers of America, Wil-
lowdale, Ontario

H. WALLACE MERRYMAN
Chairman and Chief Executive Officer, Avco
Financial Services, Inc., Newport Beach,
California

JOHN MILLER
President, National Planning Association,
Washington, D.C.

DONALD R. MONTGOMERY
Secretary-Treasurer, Canadian Labour Congress, Ottawa, Ontario

HARRY E. MORGAN, JR.
Senior Vice President, Weyerhaeuser Company, Tacoma, Washington

JOE MORRIS
President, Canadian Labour Congress, Ottawa, Ontario

*HANS HERBERT MUNTE
Executive Vice-President, International,
The Continental Group, New York, New
York

RICHARD W. MUZZY
Group Vice President — International,
Owens-Corning Fiberglas Corporation, To-
ledo, Ohio

CARL E. NICKELS, JR.
Senior Vice President, Finance and Law,
The Hanna Mining Company, Cleveland,
Ohio

HON. VICTOR deB. OLAND
Halifax, Nova Scotia

CHARLES PERRAULT
President, Perconsult Ltd., Montreal,
Quebec

RICHARD H. PETERSON
Chairman of the Board, Pacific Gas and
Electric Company, San Francisco, California

THOMAS A. REED
Group Vice President, International Control Systems, Honeywell Inc., Minneapolis, Minnesota

ROBERT J. RICHARDSON
Vice President — Finance, E. I. du Pont de Nemours & Co., Inc., Wilmington, Delaware

BEN L. ROUSE
Vice President — Business Machines Group, Burroughs Corporation, Detroit, Michigan

THOMAS W. RUSSELL, JR.
New York, New York

A. E. SAFARIAN
Professor, Department of Political Economy, University of Toronto, Toronto, Ontario

RICHARD J. SCHMEELK
Partner, Salomon Brothers, New York, New York

ARTHUR R. SEDER, JR.
Chairman and President, American Natural Resources Company, Detroit, Michigan

R. W. SPARKS
President and Chief Executive Officer, Texaco Canada Limited, Don Mills, Ontario

W. A. STRAUSS
Chairman and Chief Executive Officer, Northern Natural Gas Company, Omaha, Nebraska

ROBERT D. STUART, JR.
Chairman, The Quaker Oats Company, Chicago, Illinois

A. McC. SUTHERLAND
Director and Senior Vice President, INCO Limited, Toronto, Ontario

DWIGHT D. TAYLOR
Senior Vice President, Crown Zellerbach Corporation, San Francisco, California

W. BRUCE THOMAS
Executive Vice President—Accounting and Finance and Director, United States Steel Corporation, Pittsburgh, Pennsylvania

ALEXANDER C. TOMLINSON
Chairman of the Executive Committee, The First Boston Corporation, New York, New York

WILLIAM I. M. TURNER, JR.
President and Chief Executive Officer, Consolidated-Bathurst Limited, Montreal, Quebec

W. O. TWAITS
Toronto, Ontario

*RICHARD H. VAUGHAN
President, Northwest Bancorp, Minneapolis, Minnesota

A. O. WAY
Sr. Vice President — Finance, General Electric Company, New York, New York

WILLIAM W. WINPISINGER
President, International Association of Machinists and Aerospace Workers, Washington, D.C.

FRANCIS G. WINSPEAR
Edmonton, Alberta

D. MICHAEL WINTON
Chairman, Pas Lumber Company Limited, Minneapolis, Minnesota

GEORGE W. WOODS
President, TransCanada PipeLines, Toronto, Ontario

WILLIAM S. WOODSIDE
President, American Can Company, Greenwich, Connecticut

DON WOODWARD
International Trade Affairs Representative, National Association of Wheat Growers, Pendleton, Oregon

Honorary Members

WILLIAM DODGE
Ottawa, Ontario

CARL J. GILBERT
Dover, Massachusetts

F. PEAVEY HEFFELFINGER
Director Emeritus, Peavey Company, Minneapolis, Minnesota

HON. N. A. M. MacKENZIE
Vancouver, British Columbia

M. W. MACKENZIE
Ottawa, Ontario

HAROLD SWEATT
Honorary Chairman of the Board, Honeywell Inc., Minneapolis, Minnesota

JOHN R. WHITE
New York, New York

HENRY S. WINGATE
New York, New York

DAVID J. WINTON
Minneapolis, Minnesota

*Not a member at time of signing.

SELECTED PUBLICATIONS
OF THE CANADIAN-AMERICAN COMMITTEE*

Commercial Relations

CAC-40 *Industrial Incentive Policies and Programs in the Canadian-American Context*, by John Volpe. 1976 ($2.50)

CAC-38 *A Balance of Payments Handbook*, by Caroline Pestieau. 1974 ($2.00)

CAC-32 *Toward a More Realistic Appraisal of the Automotive Agreement*, a Statement by the Committee. 1970 ($1.00)

CAC-31 *The Canada-U.S. Automotive Agreement: An Evaluation*, by Carl E. Beigie. 1970 ($3.00)

CAC-25 *A New Trade Strategy for Canada and the United States*, a Statement by the Committee. 1966 ($1.00)

Energy and Other Resources

CAC-44 *Uranium, Nuclear Power, and Canada-U.S. Energy Relations*, by Hugh C. McIntyre. 1978 ($4.00)

CAC-41 *Coal and Canada-U.S. Energy Relations*, by Richard L. Gordon. 1976 ($3.00)

CAC-39 *Keeping Options Open in Canada-U.S. Oil and Natural Gas Trade*, a Statement by the Committee. 1975 ($1.00)

CAC-37 *Canada, the United States, and the Third Law of the Sea Conference*, by R. M. Logan. 1974 ($3.00)

CAC-36 *Energy from the Arctic: Facts and Issues*, by Judith Maxwell. 1973 ($4.00)

Investment

CAC-33 *Canada's Experience with Fixed and Flexible Exchange Rates in a North American Capital Market*, by Robert M. Dunn, Jr. 1971 ($2.00)

CAC-29 *The Performance of Foreign-Owned Firms in Canada*, by A. E. Safarian. 1969 ($2.00)

CAC-24 *Capital Flows Between Canada and the United States*, by Irving Brecher. 1965 ($2.00)

Other

CAC-43 *Agriculture in an Interdependent World: U.S. and Canadian Perspectives*, by T. K. Warley. 1977 ($4.00)

CAC-42 *A Time of Difficult Transitions: Canada-U.S. Relations in 1976*, a Staff Report. 1976 ($2.00)

CAC-35 *The New Environment for Canadian-American Relations*, a Statement by the Committee. 1972 ($1.50)

CAC-30 *North American Agriculture in a New World*, by J. Price Gittinger. 1970 ($2.00)

---

*These and other Committee publications may be ordered from the Committee's offices at 2064 Sun Life Building, Montreal, Quebec H3B 2X7, and at 1606 New Hampshire Avenue, N.W., Washington, D.C. 20009. Quantity discounts are given. A descriptive flyer of these publications is also available.